HISPANIC PARENTAL INVOLVEMENT

Title: Hispanic Parental Involvement
Subtitle: Ten Competencies Schools Need to Teach Hispanic Parents
Author: Dr. Lourdes Ferrer

Description: For years educators have known that parental involvement was a leading indicator of student success. In this book Dr. Lourdes Ferrer shares insights gained from interviews with hundreds of Hispanic students as to why their academic success is less than that of their White and Asian peers. She shares what schools can do to help Hispanic parents be involved in their children's education.

Keywords: Hispanic, Latino, parental, involvement, student, achievement, success

ISBN-13: 978-1461197638
ISBN-10: 1461197635

Publishing Prepared by: Rick Hubbard Consulting
Publishing Website: www.riverjumping.com

To contact Dr. Ferrer for permission to use these materials or to obtain information about booking her for a speaking engagement or seminar, please contact her through her websites.
www.drlourdes.net
www.thehispanicnextdoor.com

Hispanic Parental Involvement

Ten Competencies Schools
Need to Teach Hispanic Parents

By Dr. Lourdes Ferrer

THIS BOOK IS DEDICATED TO VILMA RUIZ, *MI HERMANA DEL ALMA (MY SOUL SISTER).*

Vilma,

> *We have faced so many life challenges together, and since I remember, you were always there for me. Ever since Mom passed away, we grew closer than ever. I think Mom likes that; don't you agree? From the bottom of my heart, thank you for being a mother to my three awesome children, Rebecca, Jonathan, and Deborah, and a grandmother to my three adorable grandchildren, Gabriella, Nicholas, and Zacharie. Your love and support has been unconditional. I love you, Sis! You are my angel.*

I WOULD LIKE TO RECOGNIZE RICK HUBBARD,
COMMUNICATION AND MEDIA CONSULTANT,
CONSUEGRO [MY CHILD'S FATHER IN LAW], AND LONG-
TIME FRIEND.

Consuegro Rick,

We have been friends for almost two decades. You have been my academic mentor since we met. You helped me improve my English language skills, served as a sounding board, edited every document, shared all sorts of new technologies, and advised me when making difficult academic and work-related decisions. The truth is that I would not be writing this book if it wasn't for you. While working in Palm Beach, you helped me begin the development of many of the metaphors presented in this book including, "Reading is like car jack," "Kids with character are in cruise control," "Teachers are like a GPS," and "Parents must sit in the driver's seat." I am blessed with having you by my side as I continue on my academic and professional journey.

I WOULD LIKE TO ACKNOWLEDGE THE FOLLOWING INDIVIDUALS WHO HAVE HAD A TREMENDOUS IMPACT IN MY PROFESSIONAL DEVELOPMENT. LET'S START WITH DR. LARRY DECKER, EMINENT SCHOLAR AND CHAIR OF MY DOCTORAL COMMITTEE AT FLORIDA ATLANTIC UNIVERSITY, FLORIDA.

Dr. Decker,

I was so naïve when I first started my doctoral program. I was unaware of the magnitude of the challenges I was going to face including language limitations, cultural differences, and personal problems. But I knew that with you as my advisor, I was going to succeed, no matter what. You set high expectations but always provided me with the support I needed. Thank you!

I WAS PRIVILEGED TO WORK FOR DR. MARC BARON, CHIEF OF PERFORMANCE ACCOUNTABILITY, PALM BEACH COUNTY PUBLIC SCHOOLS, FLORIDA.

Dr. Baron,

Thank you for giving me my first job as a district administrator. Do you remember how fearful I was about presenting in English to an audience of school administrators? The first time you pushed me to explain some PowerPoint slides with graphs to a crowd of principals, my legs shook like maracas. You believed in me more than I believed in myself. I learned so much about mining and analyzing data from you.

I WAS THEN BLESSED WITH WORKING FOR DR. LEE RIECK, FORMER SUPERINTENDENT OF DISTRICT 94 IN WEST CHICAGO, ILLINOIS.

Dr. Rieck,

You had a greater impact on me than you will ever know. I left the warmth of Florida for the cold of Illinois because you were determined to help Hispanic students improve their performance in school. You gave me the opportunity to study the reasons behind their lack of academic achievement. That study was the seed of this book. Because of that I gained deeper understanding about Hispanic student success; it changed my views about school reform. I will never forget your commitment to do what is right for Hispanic students.

THEN I MET DR. JUDY MINOR, ASSISTANT SUPERINTENDENT OF COMMUNITY HIGH SCHOOL, DISTRICT 99 IN DOWNERS GROVE, ILLINOIS.

Dr. Minor,

As I continued my search to understand the issues related to Hispanic academic success, you became my ally. Your professionalism and friendship empowered me to conduct the most comprehensive qualitative study I had ever done. Do you remember how much joy we had in developing programs to increase the academic achievement of the Hispanic students? You were there as I was being transformed by my interviews with the kids. You are an awesome professional and a loyal friend!

AND FINALLY, I WOULD LIKE TO ACKNOWLEDGE DR. DARLENE RUSCITTI, DuPAGE COUNTY REGIONAL SUPERINTENDENT OF SCHOOLS, ILLINOIS.

Dr. Ruscitti,

Under your bold leadership I have been able to continue finding ways to help Hispanic families reach the American Dream through academic success. Your willingness to think out-of-the-box empowers all of us who work with you to be innovative thinkers. You have given me the freedom to develop and implement programs to help schools improve the academic achievement of all their students. You have opened doors that allowed me to influence the thinking process of other educational leaders. On behalf of the students impacted by our programs, I say, "thank you!"

TABLE OF CONTENTS

Introduction 3

Competency 1: Value Kids' Education 15

Competency 2: Meet Kids' Needs 27

Competency 3: Overcome Immigrant Challenges 45

Competency 4: Maintain Family Unity 61

Competency 5: Understand Their Role 81

Competency 6: Believe in Their Children.............................. 93

Competency 7: Connect with Teachers 105

Competency 8: Make Reading a Lifestyle............................ 115

Competency 9: Make Homework a Routine.......................... 129

Competency 10: Build Kids' Character................................ 145

Closing Thoughts 155

About the Author... 161

INTRODUCTION

INTRODUCTION

¡Hola! I am Dr. Lourdes. If you are reading this, you are likely interested in learning how to engage more Hispanic parents in their children's education and to improve the learning outcomes of your Hispanic student population. Whether you are a teacher, a school administrator, or a district official, you are not alone in your interest and for good reason. Hispanics are the largest and fastest growing minority in the United States. The exponential growth and unique characteristics of this sector have brought our nation new challenges. Among the greatest of these challenges has been meeting the needs of Hispanic students. Helping these students achieve academic success is a priority in many schools' reform efforts across the nation. I wrote this book to provide you with insight and strategies for getting more Hispanic parents involved in a way that is effective and meaningful.

Hispanic is a term used to identify a wide range of ethnicities, races, and nationalities that have Spanish as their primary language. Hispanics are profoundly diverse not only in country of birth, nationality, and citizenship, but also in primary language skills, prior educational experiences, and socioeconomic and immigration status. Worldwide, Chinese is the most widely spoken language in the world, then English with Spanish a close third. The United States has the second largest Spanish-speaking community in the world, second only to Mexico.

Three generalized, but very important characteristics can describe the Hispanic culture. First, Hispanics are people who deeply value family. The family is perceived by Hispanics not only as the transmitter of the culture but also as the vehicle for achieving individual and family goals. They simply stick together!

Second, Hispanics have a very strong work ethic. They believe in hard work and appreciate the ability to provide for their families. A very common saying among Hispanics is, "Tienes que hecharle ganas al trabajo," which means, "You have to put great effort into work." Most Hispanics immigrate to the U.S. determined to work as hard as they can to improve the quality of their lives.

Third, Hispanics embrace and hold onto their faith. Their goals and aspirations are subject to God's will, and it is arrogant to think that goals can be achieved without some kind of higher power or divine intervention. One very popular expression in the Hispanic culture is "¡Si Dios quiere!" which means, "If it's God's will!" Another is "¡Ay Dios mío!" which means, "Oh my God!"

We all know that the United States is a nation of immigrants. But, I believe that the Hispanic immigration has differences from any other immigration in the history of the United States. One is in their percentage of the U.S. population. Hispanics are the largest immigration group which continues to grow in an exponential manner. According to the USA Census, Hispanics grew from almost 15 million in the 1980's to 50.5 million in our decade. They now make up 16.3% of the total USA population. The Hispanic population also accounted for most of the nation's growth, 56% from 2000 to 2010. If this growth pattern continues, we will have more than 100 million Hispanics by 2050. That is a lot of people.

Another difference is that Hispanics come from many different countries. Italian immigrants came from Italy, and the Irish came from Ireland. However, Hispanic immigrants come from more than twenty nations in Latin America - stretching from the northern border towns of Mexico to the southernmost tip of Argentina. We must not forget that there are millions who like me come from the Caribbean including Puerto Rico, Cuba, and the Dominican Republic.

Another difference with the Hispanic immigration is that many previous immigrant groups came during the Agricultural Age or Industrial Age. Their motivation, determination, and hard-work ethic opened doors to a quality life here in the United States. In contrast, the current Hispanic immigration windfall is happening in the Information Age. In these times, motivation and a strong work ethic do not necessarily lead to a quality life. In the Information Age, it is a quality education that provides the gateway to a quality life. The challenge for Hispanics is that a quality education requires mastery in academic English.

Technology plays another role with some Hispanic immigrants. It may diminish Hispanics' perceived need or desire to join the mainstream culture. Previous immigration groups had to fully leave behind the lives they had in their native countries to embrace a future here; mainstreaming or joining the "melting pot" was a matter of survival in American culture. Their native countries were too far away, visiting was too expensive, and staying in touch with their native communities was not feasible. Today's Hispanic immigrants live a different reality. Aviation is economical enough so that many can visit their native countries. The airlines shorten the time and distance. Technology allows Hispanics to stay in touch with their relatives and friends back in their countries or here in the United States. They communicate by phone, email, text, and Skype.

Additionally, our culture supports the maintenance of their native language and culture. They consume Hispanic media such as radio and TV; they utilize Spanish internet services such as using "Google" in Spanish. Technology helps provide the emotional and social support that is needed to maintain their culture for those who can use it. It is not as necessary to forsake the language and culture they left behind. Hispanics have enough numbers and enough technology to create real-world or digital communities here in the United States and around the world. They can live their entire lives somewhat separated from the mainstream American culture.

Many previous immigrants faced negative reactions from the mainstream culture. It is also true with Hispanics for some different reasons. I have personally experienced the negative stigma associated with the term Hispanic. Why? One reason is that Hispanics are over represented among people who live in poverty and participate in anti-social behaviors. There is not a day that passes without some form of bad news or negative report related to Hispanics. There are also strong anti-immigration sentiments across the nation, and the term "Hispanic" is associated with illegal immigrants. Our current national financial crisis amplifies this because Hispanics are perceived as more of a burden on society rather than people who will strengthen our nation.

A negative perception of Hispanics is intensified because they are doing poorly academically. Hispanic youth are the most under-educated major segment of the population. In every national and state standardized test, Hispanic students' scores lag behind their White and Asian peers in mathematics, reading, and science. Today Hispanics have the highest drop-out rate. Only 57% of Hispanic students graduate from high school, and barely 10% earn a college degree. This definitely affects their employability. Because of the size of this population, the lack of academic achievement also has a wide-reaching effect on the country. It weakens the nation's competiveness in the world markets.

Many of these students may not reach their potential if they attend schools with environments that are not conducive to learning. As an experienced mathematics teacher and district administrator, I know Hispanic students are likely to attend schools characterized by poor instruction, lower academic expectations, and disciplinary problems. These same schools are likely to be staffed by teachers who are not qualified or lack the preparation to teach traditional academic content to non-traditional students, those who might not be proficient in English or need remediation because of their poor academic background.

These conditions compelled me to study why such performance gaps existed between Hispanics and their White and Asian counterparts. I learned so much reading from the experts regarding the achievement gaps. I also drew upon my personal insights as a Hispanic immigrant, mother, school teacher, and district administrator. By 2006, I felt the need to develop a deeper understanding of the reasons behind these on-going performance gaps. I decided to learn from the kids themselves; in the end, they are the ones who answer the questions on the states' tests that are used to evaluate the schools' improvement efforts. If we want them to excel, why not ask them why they don't?

That's what I have done for the past five years. I used group and individual interviews in which I have continually asked hundreds of Hispanic middle and high school students the following questions: Why are the Hispanic students' scores on state accountability tests lower than their White and Asian peers? Why are Hispanic students under-represented in Honors or Advanced Placement (AP) math and science courses? Why do so many Hispanics not graduate from high school or graduate with a weakened academic foundation? I asked these questions to Hispanic students in many states across the nation including Florida, California, and Illinois. I was bewildered with their responses!

Most of the students' responses to these questions had little or nothing to do with what happened in their classrooms or schools. Words such as "parents," "family," and "home" outweighed words such as "teacher," "classroom," or "school." I was surprised to see that their reasons for the Hispanic student poor performance in school were usually linked, directly or indirectly, to the lack of parental support or involvement. What these students shared with me changed my views towards school improvement and my professional practice.

In general, Hispanic students believed their parents' involvement was more powerful in helping them achieve academic success than any school or teacher intervention. There is no doubt that Hispanic parents love their children; they demonstrated their love by leaving behind everything they knew to provide their children an opportunity for a better future here in the United States. The challenge is that many parents, as one of the students said, "Don't know how to navigate the American Educational System and do not know how to know." The problem is a lack of knowledge and a lack of knowledge about how to get the knowledge. The problem is not the lack of love.

Listen to what students said in their own words. One student observed, "My parents are more than happy if I just finish high school. It does not matter which classes I take, as long as I pass. They are not really expecting me to go to college, or anything like that. They just want me to work and help out."

Students wished more parents believed in their children's ability to learn and did not judge their children based on their own personal experiences. A young man commented, "My father failed in school when he was little. He just attended elementary school and then went straight to work. I think he thinks that because I am his son the same thing will happen to me."

Students also believe their parents do not really know the role they need to play in their children's education. Their parents are likely to believe that they are doing what they are supposed to be doing by providing shelter, food, and sending them to school. The students consistently express that they are pretty much on their own. Things like which courses to take, how to apply for college, how to prepare for a college entrance test, or how get financial aid was pretty much the student's responsibility. As a student put it, "White students get a lot of help from their parents. Their parents went to school here, and they know a lot of stuff about school and what to do to go to college. Hispanics have to explain everything to their parents."

Another student expressed another concern, "I feel like, divided. In school everything is in English and at home everything is in Spanish. I have to be one way at school and another way at home." They said they feel "trapped between two worlds." They learn to master all sorts of technological devices when their parents can "hardly turn on a computer." Many of them had already reached higher levels of education than their parents. And some of the students were born citizens while their parents were undocumented. Parents can't monitor their kids' education because of their lower academic background and were too computer illiterate to even monitor their progress online. Some students worry greatly about their parents' illegal immigration status, "I am afraid, most of the time, not knowing if my parents will be home tonight. If they are deported, what am I going to do?"

Many of the students believe that their parents were not connected with their teachers due to their parents' lack of English proficiency. In many cases, a certain level of mistrust and discomfort exists. "White parents come to school and ask questions like they have the right to do so. My parents don't feel that way. Another thing is that they feel kind of inferior because they never finished school."

Referring to their White and Asian peers, one Hispanic student said, "They have the habit of reading because they have been reading since they were babies. So having to read a whole chapter and then answer all the questions is not a big deal for them. I struggle with every line. It is too hard and I give up and that affects my grades."

A surprising comment a student made was, "I wish my parents had taught me to be more responsible with school work since I was little. They just work hard and then come home really tired. We talk about other stuff: family, money problems, and all that; but not about stuff like being responsible and persistent with school work. I guess that if I show up to school every day, that's good enough for them."

There was consensus among the students that the greatest sources of stress and frustration were the lack of understanding of the language and culture, other people's negative perceptions towards Hispanics, and the illegal residential status.

Students expressed that they were overwhelmed with their parents' hopelessness and powerlessness when facing challenges that result from immigrating to this country. Their parents' struggles became their struggles; that did not allow them to focus in school. With a gloomy face one high school student said, "It is hard for me to sit in class and pay attention. My mind wonders. All I think is about is my parents. I wish I could help." Many students who participated in one-on-one interviews simply broke down in tears!

The students in my studies confirmed what experts in the field of education have stated for decades: parental involvement is one of the leading indicators of students' academic achievement. We know that when parents are involved, students improve their academic achievement regardless the economic, racial, or family and cultural background.

To increase the academic achievement of Hispanic students, we must invest time, energy, and resources to get more Hispanic parents involved in their children's education. We must continue our efforts to improve our schools, but just holding teachers and administrators accountable for their Hispanic student performance will not give us the results we seek. It takes parental support. What is it that we need Hispanic parents to know and be able to do to better support their kids' education? That is what this book is about.

My personal experience as an immigrant, parent, teacher, administrator, and consultant added to the voices of hundreds of Hispanic students across the nation, helped me identify ten competencies that parents must demonstrate to better support their children's education. Each chapter covers one competency. These competencies provide you with a framework for developing a solid parental involvement program.

The same way that life experiences are not independent from each other, the content of some of the chapters will overlap with the content of others. For example, in Chapter 3, the lack of English proficiency is discussed as a challenge that parents face when they immigrate into the United States, and then, in Chapter 4, it is presented as one of the five gaps that contribute to the family-divide. Since it took me almost three years to write this book, every chapter reflects a perspective unique to a specific time in my journey of understanding.

CHAPTER 1

COMPETENCY # 1: VALUE KIDS' EDUCATION

Parents embrace and manifest the belief that a quality education leads to a quality life.

"I want to help my race, and I want to help my community. I want to be part of something, you know, so I can have a better life. In Mexico, there are not many opportunities. My mom came here to give us an opportunity and, if we don't take it, it is like giving up all the sacrifice she did. It is like letting her down. I want to have a good life." – Tito, Hispanic High School Student

COMPETENCY # 1: VALUE KIDS' EDUCATION

Why do so many Hispanics immigrate to the United States? The answer: They love their children and want to provide them with an opportunity for a better future. The Pew Hispanic Institute reports that 75% of older Hispanics expect that their children will have a better financial future than themselves. That is the main reason why they immigrated to the United States in the first place. However, many of them believe that working hard is the key to success. While they may value hard work, by itself, hard work will not ensure a better future.

Hispanic parents need to value education because, more than ever before, a quality education is the doorway to a quality life in the United States. This is why I believe that the first competency Hispanic parents need to learn is to value their kids' education. It is imperative that parents embrace and then manifest the belief that a quality education leads to a quality life. In the United States, a quality education is the door that opens opportunities to a quality life.

There are four ideas that parents must internalize in order to embrace and manifest the belief that the pathway to a quality life is through a quality education. Parents must first understand what a quality education is as well as what constitutes a quality life in American mainstream culture. They must also know that just attending school or graduating high school does not guarantee the best possible quality of education. Ultimately, we must help parents understand the correlation that exists between the level of quality education their kids receive and the future quality of life their kids will experience.

A QUALITY EDUCATION

Parents need a practical understanding of what a quality education is to know if their children are receiving the best schooling available. The problem is that the meaning of a quality education is not static. If you have been in the field of education for three decades or more (like me), you know that the meaning of a quality education has changed, and continues to change based on the knowledge and skills students need to earn a decent living at a given place and time.

Today a quality education means that students should acquire the knowledge and the skills they need to be competent in two very important core subject areas - reading and mathematics. Why reading and mathematics? Students who are competent readers are better able to become independent life-long learners - a vital skill in our constantly changing society. Additionally, students competent in mathematics are better equipped with critical-thinking and problem-solving skills, abilities that are needed to face all sorts of life challenges. It is for these reasons, and many others, that the No Child Left Behind (NCLB) Act sets expectations that all children demonstrate proficiency in reading and mathematics as determined by state accountability tests.

Too many Hispanic parents are not aware that the Federal

government holds schools accountable for educational proficiency in both core areas for all students. This proficiency is irrespective of race, ethnicity, socio-economic status, or learning disabilities; it includes their children. Every Hispanic parent should be informed about this law and the impact it has on the American educational system. They need to understand its importance and the meaning of what constitutes reading and mathematics proficiency.

When I was a little girl, a good reader was a person who could decode symbols, pronounce words, and read sentences with a certain level of fluency. If you could "read lines," then you were considered proficient in reading. But now we have to go beyond just reading lines; we have to read "between lines" and "above lines." What do I mean by this? Reading proficiency now requires a higher level of analytical comprehension. This means that given any written passage, students must be able to uncover the purpose of the author; for example, is the purpose to persuade or to inform? Students must determine the meaning of the words within the context. They must also be able to infer and predict based on the information provided in the text.

When first-graders read the story of "The Three Little Pigs," the teacher is likely to ask, "If you had a chance to speak to the first little pig, what advice would you give him?" Or "What do you think this story is trying to teach us?" In contrast, a few decades ago, the teacher could have asked, "How many pigs were in the story?" Or "What materials did each pig use to build his house?" Hispanic parents will not understand this shift unless we intentionally explain it to them.

Now let's consider what it means to be proficient in mathematics. Remember the old days when mathematics teachers would say, "You need to learn math so you can balance your checking account." (By the way, for many years, I was one of "those" teachers; I used the "balancing your checkbook" example to help my students see the usefulness of mathematics.) Those days are over, and parents must know that. Today, students are required to go beyond simple computations and basic mathematical algorithms. They must also use critical thinking and problem solving processes to find the solutions to math problems in different contexts.

Some decades ago we asked sixth-graders to find the volume of a 12" by 4" by 5" box; or, the volume of a cylinder with a radius of 1" and a height of 5". Teachers today expect sixth graders to answer, "How many cans of 1" radius and a 5" height can be fit in a 12" by 5" by 4" box? Or "How big does the box need to be if the amount of cans is doubled, tripled, etc.?

Parents must become aware that high school students who master reading and mathematics are less likely to drop out of school and more likely to pursue a post-secondary education. When I speak to them, I let them know that high school graduates receive greater earnings upon entering the workforce. I emphatically tell Hispanic parents that reaching proficiency in reading and mathematics is not an option! Parents must closely monitor their children's education and ensure that their children are at or above grade level in reading and mathematics.

ATTENDANCE, GRADUATION, AND MORE

A challenge we face as educators is the Hispanic parents' perception that just attending school, moving up grade levels, or even graduating high school, guarantees a quality education. Good attendance and high school graduation definitely helps, but they are not the only criteria for judging if a student's education constitutes a quality education. Quality education prepares students for more.

Too many Hispanic students move up the grade-level ladder with reading and mathematics skills that are significantly below their grade levels. It is common knowledge in educational circles that by fourth grade the average Hispanic student is reading two grade levels behind the average White student. By 12th grade, the average Hispanic student performs in math and reading at the same level as the average eighth grade White student. This is happening with the Hispanic students who stay in school through graduation. This is unacceptable, and I guarantee you that most Hispanic parents are not aware of these facts.

Educators must help Hispanic parents understand that, in today's economy, students must pursue some kind of education after graduation. I teach high school students that the days when a high school diploma was a "big deal" are over. Eighty percent of the fastest-growing jobs in the United States require a technical, vocational, or college education. It comes back to a quality education because most careers require students to be skilled readers and have a solid foundation in mathematics.

Even if they graduate from high school and enroll in college, students who lack reading and mathematics skills are more likely to end up taking remedial courses in college - learning what they should have learned when they were in high school. Many of them grow discouraged and quit college before the end of their first year. They lack the motivation to overcome the enormous challenges occurring because of their reading and mathematics deficiencies. Let me illustrate this with a personal story.

I graduated from high school in my home town of Bayamón, Puerto Rico with a Grade Point Average (GPA) of 4.0 points. Growing up in a very impoverished environment, a local community college was my only choice. Like any high school student, I took the College Entrance Board Test. I got accepted to the closest community college, the Colegio Regional de Bayamón. I will never forget the shock I felt my first day on the college campus, looking at my schedule and realizing that most of my courses were different from those of my peers from private schools. They were taking Mathematics 101, and I was taking Mathematics 001. I had several 001 classes instead of 101's. I was alarmed! I immediately requested a meeting with one of the counselors, something I had never done. I do not think we even had those "fancy" services in my school.

I asked the counselor, "Why are my core subjects 001 instead of 101 like my peers?" And her response was: "Your College Entrance Board test scores were way too low. Even though you have a 4.00 GPA, the test results show that you are not ready for college courses - at least not yet. Those 001 courses will prepare you for the college-level courses you will hopefully take next year. Lourdes, you need to beef up your reading and mathematics skills."

I was so disappointed with myself! How is that possible with a 4.0 GPA? How had I performed so low in the reading and mathematics portions of the test? My experience illustrates that just attending school and graduating high school does not guarantee a quality education. I never took an Honors or Advanced Placement (AP) course. I graduated high school without ever taking courses such as Algebra II or Chemistry. By personal experience, I know that just attending school and graduating high school does not necessarily prepare students for a post-secondary education.

We must teach Hispanic parents how to monitor their children's academic careers. Parents must know if their children read and do math at or above grade level. They must play a role in helping their children master these two core academic areas. It is their responsibility to make sure that their kids' education prepares them for a post-secondary education and for life.

A Quality Life

Parents must also develop a better understanding of the meaning of a quality life in the United States. During workshops for Hispanic parents, I usually asked, "What is a quality life for you?" Or, "How do you reach that quality life?" I soon learned that the beliefs of many parents are different from the beliefs generally held by Americans in the mainstream culture, especially among newly-arrived immigrants.

Americans generally believe that a quality life goes beyond having financial stability. A quality life also includes having a healthy mind and body, strong and supportive relationships, freedom in defining one's own destiny, and opportunities to leave a legacy.

Financial stability allows people to provide for themselves and their families. Financial stability also provides one with some of the pleasures of life, which is considered fundamental in the U.S. society. People with healthy minds and bodies have the greater ability to focus when thinking and, therefore, have greater potential to learn. People who have strong and supportive relationships are surrounded by people they can trust, with whom to share their ideas and explore solutions to difficult problems. Strong and supportive relationships are essential in the pursuit of significant goals. People with the freedom to define their own life paths can create life options for themselves and turn their dreams into realities. And finally, people who have the opportunity to leave a legacy can go beyond pursuing their own and their love one's happiness and make a difference in the lives of others. In more than 30 years of working with the Hispanic community, I have learned that many have a very different idea concerning a quality life.

A significant number of Hispanic parents are accepting or even satisfied with situations that mainstream Americans might consider insufficient or unacceptable. Some Hispanics see successes in situations that might be considered by others as failures.

For example, I often hear high school teachers, especially those who teach English as a Second Language (ESL), complain about their students' lack of interest in participating in Advanced Placement (AP) courses and extra-curricular activities that could enhance student learning and provide greater academic opportunities. On the other hand, I hear many of their ESL students, especially the ones who lived in extreme poverty back in their native countries, openly express contentment with the following standards of accomplishment.

- First, they live in the United States of America, which alone is a huge success!

- Second, they have enough English language skills to find a part-time job and make more money than their parents did back in their native countries.

- Third, they will soon graduate from an American high school, which will make them the first ones in their families to do so.

Subjectively, all these are huge successes. In their minds they have already succeeded. They feel they are living a quality life! During a series of interviews that I conducted in one Illinois high school, a senior high school student revealed his perspective of success.

He said, "Dr. Lourdes, for me, being here in the United States it is like being born again. It is like a dream come true; a new opportunity that life has given me. I speak English...I already make more money than my parents did back in Mexico. I will be the first in my family to graduate. When I someday go back, they (family and friends in Mexico) will see the difference."

In America a Quality Education Does Lead to a Quality Life

The final challenge that we face when helping Hispanic parents value education is to convince them that a good education is the door to opportunities for a quality life in the United States. You see, many Hispanic parents come from countries where this is not necessarily true. Where they are from, education does not necessarily open doors to an improved life style. Who their parents are, or what their families' financial resources are, plays a much larger role in determining what doors are open for them.

For several years, I did community development in Central America. I saw many qualified professionals, medical doctors, lawyers, and others working in low-skill, low-paying jobs. These countries were in desperate need of these professionals, but, for societal reasons, there was not the financial infrastructure to employ them. The college graduates who got the good jobs were more likely the ones that, in one way or another, were connected with those in power.

It's said, "Who your parents are and not who you are, is what is going to get your foot in the door." It is for this reason that many of the Hispanic parents, who enroll their children in our public schools, but belonged to a lower socio-economic class back in their countries of origin, might not see education as the gateway to quality life. Upward financial and social mobility is not part of their frame of reference.

More than anything else, Hispanic parents must understand that things are different in the U.S. There are great opportunities for upward social and economic mobility through a quality education. If they understand that correlation, they are more likely to value their kids' education and support it.

While what I have shared in this chapter might not apply to all immigrants, it does apply to many newer Hispanic immigrants, especially parents with a low academic background. We know that they love their children. One of the reasons why they immigrated to the United States is to provide their children an opportunity for a better future. That is why we need to help them understand that a quality education, here in the United States, is the door to opportunities for a quality life. I promise you, they will be motivated to do what is necessary to help their children achieve academic success. They will learn to value education. They will surely embrace and manifest the belief that a quality education is the door to a quality life.

CHAPTER 2

COMPETENCY # 2: MEET KIDS' NEEDS

Parents are able to meet their children's physical, emotional and social needs within the context of the American mainstream culture.

"It seems like no one cares enough to take the time to listen. Most of us see it as it began with us being beneath the White man and that most of us aren't going to amount to anything. Personally, I can't concentrate on my school work. My parents are working all day, and I miss a lot of school because somebody has to take care of my baby brother. My brother, who is older than me, works like forty hour a week to help pay the bills. My mom says that family always goes first." - Juanita, Hispanic High School Student

COMPETENCY # 2: MEET KIDS' NEEDS

It is very difficult, if not impossible, for children to learn and achieve academic success if their parents are not able to meet their children's basic physical, emotional, and social needs. Because we are physical, emotional, and social beings, meeting these needs is an important part of a child's total development and, therefore, a vital component of the parental role. Parents should take this responsibility seriously. I believe that the parents' ability to meet their children's basic human necessities, as defined by and within the context of the mainstream American culture, must be one of the competencies they must demonstrate.

Parents need to develop a better understanding of what their children's basic needs are. They must also become aware of the transformational life processes they are likely to experience while meeting their children's' need in the context of a new culture. I always teach Hispanic immigrant parents that like caterpillars become butterflies, we must be transformed.

CHILDREN'S BASIC PHYSICAL, EMOTIONAL, AND SOCIAL NEEDS

Let's start with physical needs. It seems obvious that good quality air, a nutritious diet, plenty of exercise, and suitable shelter are some of the basic physical needs of children. Good quality air promotes robust mental functioning and impedes the spread of airborne diseases. A nutritious diet promotes total health and deters many illnesses. Exercise encourages optimal physical development and promotes a feeling of well-being. An appropriate shelter, among many things, protects children from unsuitable environmental and physical conditions that could endanger their lives. Parents must be able to meet these needs in order for their children to develop properly and learn. However, meeting these basic physical needs is not enough. There are emotional needs that also need to be met.

Parents must be taught that affection, discipline, a sense of belonging, and encouragement are a few of the many emotional needs that children have. Affection is simply love. Children need to feel loved. Children also need discipline in their lives. They must understand that parents discipline their children out of love and responsibility for their proper upbringing. Children also need to experience a sense of belonging. They need to feel they belong in their family and are not simply an accident. Like any of us, children also need encouragement. They need to feel good about who they are and believe that determination will allow them to overcome any challenge they will face in life. Children are better positioned to reach their life potential when parents are able to meet their emotional needs.

We cannot thrive in isolation. We have been "wired" to be part of something bigger than ourselves. Parents need to be aware that their children have social needs. Many parents, not limited to Hispanics, are not aware of these needs. Communicating socially, peer acceptance, significant relationships, and meaningful involvement are just a few of the social needs that children have.

Parents must learn how to teach their children effective social communication. Children must be able to clearly express, verbally and non-verbally, their ideas and feelings. Children need to feel accepted, not only by their parents and siblings, but also by their peers. Children need to establish meaningful relationships with non-family members. Although the family plays an important social role in the life of a child, these relationships alone do not suffice children's social needs. They need friends. Kids also need to be involved in such a way that they can make significant contributions in their social circles. If absent from their parents, siblings or peers, they want to be missed. Children have a better chance to achieve academic success when their parents are able to provide for their social needs.

TRANSFORMATIONAL PROCESSES IMMIGRANTS FAMILIES GO THROUGH

What are the transformational processes that many immigrant parents might go through while meeting basic needs in the context of the mainstream culture? In particular, what obstacles might immigrant parents face in those processes? I have spent most of my life in Latin America, not only in Puerto Rico, but also in Guatemala, Mexico, and Honduras. Life can be very different in those countries. By experience I know that when Hispanic families immigrate into the United States,

they have to adjust and learn how to provide for their kids' needs in a new environment. Not only might the physical environment be different, but also the beliefs, values, and standards that determine how these physical, emotional and social needs must be met. Like caterpillars go through a changing process to become butterflies, leaving the cocoon to venture into unknown open air, immigrant parents must be transformed to meet their kids' needs in the context of a new culture.

I have identified three significant parallel transformational processes that Hispanic immigrant family will experience while meeting their children's needs in the context of the mainstream American culture. These processes are:

1. Moving from a family-centric to a child-centric cultural paradigm;
2. Moving up the ladder of the grief-acculturation process; and,
3. Developing a better understanding of the American mainstream culture.

PROCESS # 1: MOVING FROM A FAMILY-CENTRIC TO A CHILD-CENTRIC CULTURAL PARADIGM

Moving from a family-centric to a child-centric paradigm is the foremost process most Hispanic families go through to successfully attend to their kids' needs in the context of the new culture. This process stems from divergences in two different frames of reference and requires a paradigm shift for parents. The family-centric paradigm is prevalent in the Hispanic culture while a child-centric paradigm is prevalent in the American mainstream culture. The fundamental difference between these two cultural paradigms is where the focus of attention lies. The family-centric norms focus on the well-being of the family; it is communal and answers the question, "What is best for the family?" On the other hand, the child-centric frame of reference focuses on the child; it is individualistic and answers the question, "What is best for the child?"

The family plays such an important role in the Hispanic culture that individual family members, including children, are likely to:

- View themselves as family-members more than as individuals.
- Perceive family well-being and satisfaction as a measure of their personal successes.
- Subordinate their desires, goals or needs to those of their families.
- Be dependent upon and compliant toward their parents, grandparents, aunts, and uncles.
- Revere generational wisdom for guidance and acculturation.
- Rely on their families rather than on external institutions when facing life challenges.

As a first-generation, Hispanic woman, I would say that all the above cultural characteristics are honorable. However, they can also deter parents from meeting their children's basic needs in this country. In the U.S., what is best for the child as an individual is generally the focus of any family decision-making process. People might not view Latino parents as adequate providers if they do not learn to see their children as individuals rather than just as part of their families. Hispanic parents may need encouragement to teach their children to pursue their own dreams, become independent, make their own decisions, and take responsibility for their own actions. Allow me to give you examples that demonstrate the differences between these two life paradigms.

The first example is that of Hispanic parents expecting their children to be interpreters. Imagine a fifth grade girl who is absent from school because she was interpreting for her mother at the women's clinic. I have seen it happen again and again! The fact that at that young age and in that context, she was able to move from one language to another is admirable. At the same time, I believe that we should not employ children as interpreters. They do not have the cognitive or emotional maturity to be exposed to information that is intended for adults. What is best for that family might be to have its own interpreter and not depend on an outsider. Nevertheless, what is best for that child is to be protected from information and experiences that could damage her emotional stability. A fifth grade girl is better off in school learning with her peers than at the clinic learning firsthand about her mother's health issues.

The second example is when parents overly depend upon their children to take care of younger siblings during and after school hours. As a mathematics high school teacher, I dealt with Latino girls who missed my class or a test because they stayed home taking care of their younger siblings. I know too many high schools that struggle with getting a greater Hispanic representation in their after school extra-curricular programs because their Latino students, especially the girls, cannot stay after school. These girls not only miss the benefits of participating in extra-curricular activities, but they are so tired after taking care of their younger siblings that they do not have the time or the energy to do their homework, which has a negative impact in their academic performance. What is best for the family might be having its own in-house babysitter. Nevertheless, what is best for those Latina girls is to become involved with their peers in extra-curricular activities and have ample time and energy to comply with homework responsibilities.

The last example that I would like to give is that of parents depending on their teenage children, especially the boys, to support their families. One of the most important reasons why so many Latino high school boys drop out of school is because they decide to work full time. They do not hold full time jobs to buy the latest fashions, but to help their parents pay the electrical, gas, or other utility bills. When teaching high school mathematics, I remember losing so many of my

male students because of this. What is best for their families was to have one more income to help support the entire family. Nevertheless, what is best for those male students is to stay in school, graduate, and enroll in a post-secondary program that could ensure a better job.

PROCESS # 2: MOVING UP THE LADDER OF THE GRIEF-ACCULTURATION PROCESS

The second process that immigrant parents go through, while trying to meet their children's needs within the context of the American culture, is moving up the ladder of the unavoidable grief-acculturation process. What I mean by a grief-acculturation process is that while going through some of the stages of acculturation, the immigrant parents and their children experience many of the emotions people undergo when they grieve other losses.

Most of us are aware of how difficult and painful it is for people to lose a loved one. We also empathize with any person who is going through the process of divorce. We feel sorry for people who lose their jobs. We become concerned when people lose their homes. On the other hand, few people are aware of how difficult and painful it is for immigrants to leave their countries, cultures, languages, relatives, communities, friends, and everything that was known to them to venture into a new "world." It is like dying to be born again! The only thing that immigrants bring with them, besides a few pieces of clothing, is "la esperanza de un futuro mejor;" which means, "a hope for a better future."

I have conducted numerous studies across the nation to find

out from the Hispanic high school students' perspectives the reasons behind their lack of achievement in school and low-test scores on their states' accountability tests. During these studies, hundreds of Latino students have opened their hearts and shared with me the difficulties and pain they have gone through while adapting to this country. Immigration is a long, difficult, and painful process for parents and their children. Let's go over the stages of acculturation and how each intertwines with grief.

During the first stage of acculturation, immigrant families are likely to experience euphoria, called "The Honeymoon Period." During this period, which only lasts a short time, individuals are in love with the newness of their surroundings and jubilant for the opportunity they have ahead of them – the hope to improve the quality of their lives. Like one Latino high school student once said to me, "I see coming here to the United States as a second opportunity life has given me to reach my dreams." However, this "in love" and "thrilled" first stage is followed by "The Cultural Shock Period," the second stage of acculturation.

During this second stage, individuals start longing for the relatives and friends they left behind in their native countries. They notice and are shocked by the huge differences that exist between their native cultures and the mainstream culture of this country. They feel deprived of everything that was familiar to them, which creates a sense of loss. It is during this stage that the first surges of grieving "kick in."

This perceived sense of loss might last for several months. Like individuals in a mourning process, they might experience disorientation, depression, withdrawal, fear, anxiety, and loneliness. This stage can be more problematic and painful when immigrants also feel unwelcomed or experience discrimination.

I have a better understanding now of this second stage of acculturation than when I immigrated into the United States almost two decades ago. Rebecca, my oldest daughter, and I had a deep and long conversation about the grief of this acculturation stage.

"Mom, I was only twelve when we moved to the United States. It was such a difficult time in my life. I was sick to my stomach every day. I don't even know how I made it without some kind of counseling or medication because I am sure I was depressed."

During that conversation, we both remembered how unhappy she was. She longed for everything she left behind in Guatemala, where she was raised. She did not enjoy her high school years and could hardly wait until her high school graduation day. Looking back, after all these years, what really bothers me now is that I was not there for her, at least not emotionally. I was too busy going through my own grieving process. I was also experiencing a cultural shock. We were both immersed in a deep sense of loss.

This is why it is so important that school administrators, teachers, guidance counselors, psychologists, and those who work in schools with high percentages of Latino immigrants become aware of the emotional distress immigrants go through. Understanding, I believe, must precede any outreach effort on the school part.

After going through "The Cultural Shock Period," immigrants are likely to enter the stage known as "The Cultural Stress Period." During this stage, Hispanic immigrant families gradually start to recover an emotional equilibrium. As in the mourning process, individuals acknowledge and accept the life changes from the loss of the life they once knew. Life is going to be different from now on, so they must learn to deal with the changes. They seek realistic solutions to the problems posed by adapting to a new country and culture without many of the relatives they left behind. They must reconstruct themselves. It is during this stage that immigrants, especially students, could experience the stress of an identity crisis.

La India María, a popular Hispanic comedian, conveys this same idea by saying, "Yo no soy ni de aquí, ni de allá. Yo no sé Inglés y se me está olvidando el Español." In English she is saying, "I am not from here, nor I am from there. I do not know English, and I am forgetting my Spanish." It is during this stage that immigrant family members feel neither bound firmly to their native cultures nor adapted to the new American mainstream culture.

Once the phase of "The Cultural Stress Period" is over, the immigrant enters the last acculturation stage, "The Adaptation Period." As in the mourning progression the individual lets go of the past and holds on to the future. This stage is an extremely important period in the process of acculturation because it is here that the immigrant is either assimilated or acculturated. When individuals are acculturated, they are able to find value and meaning in both cultures and can identify with both. Students, in particular, are able to react positively towards both cultures and no longer feel the need to hide their linguistic and cultural background. However, when assimilated, which is not the ideal outcome, the individual's home culture is replaced by

the new culture. Students, in particular, usually over identify with the new culture and might deny their cultural and linguistic background. I must clarify that assimilation is likely to have negative implications for an immigrant student's family. Students who move in this direction experience low self-esteem and confidence.

School leaders, teachers, and other professionals who work with the Hispanic community will be empowered to better serve this population if they become aware of the stages and the grieving process that is intertwined in those stages.

Process # 3: Developing a better understanding of the American mainstream culture

The third process Hispanic immigrant families must undergo while they meet their children's needs within the context of the mainstream culture is developing a better understanding of the American mainstream culture. You and I know that culture is more than the food people eat, the clothes they wear, or the music they play.

People who eat "tacos" are not necessarily from Mexico nor are people who dance Salsa necessarily from Puerto Rico.

What is culture then? Culture is a shared frame of reference for interacting with and interpreting the world in which people live. In other words, culture shapes the way people communicate and relate with each other and determines how people perceive their life experiences.

The three greatest components of any culture are the language (verbal and non-verbal), values, and beliefs. The inability to navigate these components has a negative impact on the Hispanic parents' ability to meet their children's basic needs in accordance with societal norms. I know from experience that not being able to communicate in English effectively is the greatest obstacle an immigrant parent will face in the United States.

During one of my parent workshops, a Latino dad said to me, "Dr. Lourdes, I feel handicapped. I hear words and sounds, but do not understand what they mean. I know what I want to say, but I do not have the words to say it."

In another parent workshop, a mom said to me, "I am so embarrassed, Dr. Lourdes. Years have passed by, and I still can't speak English well. I don't understand what is wrong with me. I even became a citizen and passed that test. I am a citizen of this country and still can't communicate in English. What can I do?"

This language limitation is a great source of frustration and stress, and a barrier parents must overcome in order to provide for their kids' most basic needs. Suppose that a small child gets sick in the middle of the night, and his parents take him to the emergency room. It will be very difficult for the hospital personnel to provide adequate services when parents do not have the language skills to explain what is wrong with the child in the first place.

I do not waste any opportunity when I am addressing a Hispanic audience. I always ask, individually or as a group, "How is your English, Sir?" or "How many years have you been in this country?" I do not accept excuses! If they can't communicate in English at a level that they can provide for their children's basic needs, then they must go to school to learn it and put in place strategies that accelerate the language acquisition process, period.

People's beliefs are definitely behind their actions. For example, most people in the mainstream culture do not believe that physical punishment is an acceptable way to discipline a child. Causing any physical pain to a child can be considered child abuse, even when it is done to improve or modify a child's behavior. There are acceptable ways for disciplining children such as not letting them play with their favorite toys, watch their favorite TV shows, or participate in their favorite activities. On the other hand, many Latino parents come from cultures believing in giving "una buena paliza," that is, a good beating, to a child is the best way to get a child to behave properly. This kind of discipline practice will definitely get parents into trouble with the law. In this country, a "buena paliza" is considered child abuse.

Hispanic parents will have a hard time parenting their children in this culture if they don't understand and embrace the beliefs that are at the foundation of the American society. I believe that any curricular program for Hispanic parental involvement should include teaching the beliefs embedded in the mainstream culture. It can help them internalize and exhibit behaviors that lead to a successful acculturation.

Over time, Hispanic parents must embrace many of the values of the mainstream culture. What people value, or perceive as important, is the focal point and at the core, of their lives. Hispanic parents must not only understand but eventually embrace many of the values of the new culture.

When I travel, I see many parents using the time before boarding a plane to read to their children or ask them about what they read. When I shop, I see parents teaching their kids how to read labels and why certain foods are healthier than others. My point is that education is valued so much in U. S. that every moment is likely to become a teaching moment.

On the other hand, because many Hispanic parents come from countries in which education does not provide equality nor does it provide freedom to choose a life path, education is not valued as it is valued here in the United States.

Hispanic parents must meet their kids' basic needs, but they must learn to do it as defined by and within the context of mainstream American culture. It will take time! I know personally that it can take several years for an immigrant parent to go through the process embracing, at least partially, a child-centric versus a family-centric life paradigm. It may also take several years to successfully move up the ladder of the grief-acculturation process. Developing a better understanding of the American mainstream culture will require acquiring the language and embracing the beliefs and values at the core of the new culture. This will also take time. Let's be prepared to show understanding and patience while we are helping them parent their children in the new "world" they voluntarily decided to embrace.

CHAPTER 3

COMPETENCY # 3: OVERCOME IMMIGRANT CHALLENGES

Parents overcome the challenges their families encounter because of immigrating into the United States.

"Stereotypes tend to keep Hispanics from living to their fullest potential. Many Hispanics are used to being looked down upon. So living with the words of oppression and the reminder of stereotypes keeps me from falling. I am Latina. I want to make something of myself. I want to prove everyone else wrong." – Lucia, Hispanic High School Student

COMPETENCY # 3: OVERCOME IMMIGRANT CHALLENGES

Every time I offer a seminar about Hispanic parental involvement, I passionately and with great conviction state that Hispanic parents love their children so much that they were willing to leave their homelands, culture, extended families, community, and everything familiar to them in order to provide their children an opportunity for a better future. Parents were willing to sacrifice because of love.

That was the reason that motivated me to travel to the United States. I wanted my three children, Rebecca, Jonathan, and Deborah (who at that time were 12, 10 and 4) to be educated in this country. I dreamed about the idea that they could reach proficiency in the English language, graduate from an American high school, go to college, earn a degree and, most of all, live a quality life. I was determined! Nevertheless, I knew I was going to face challenges I had never faced before. Still, my dream to provide my children with an opportunity to have a better life continued to fuel me to move forward and to face the battle.

CHALLENGES HISPANIC IMMIGRANT FAMILIES FACE

Parents who are aware of the challenges that their families will encounter because of immigrating to the U.S. are in a better position to help their families overcome these challenges and in a better situation to monitor and supervise their children's education. Hispanic parents' ability to mitigate the impact of leaving behind the life they knew and venture into an unfamiliar culture is the third competency Hispanic parents need to learn.

Like eagles, immigrant parents must use the winds that their challenges bring as stepping stones to fly even higher. In my opinion, the four greatest challenges the Hispanic immigrant family is likely to face are:

1. The lack of proficiency in the English language;
2. The misalignment between the two cultures;
3. Adverse opinions and behaviors toward Hispanics, and,
4. An undocumented immigration status.

CHALLENGE # 1: THE LACK OF ENGLISH PROFICIENCY

I touched on the lack of proficiency in the English language in the last chapter, but let's look at this issue more deeply. Hispanics who immigrate to the United States often lack the English language skills that are necessary to obtain and retain a job, locate a place to live, enroll their children in school and accomplish the mundane tasks that adults are accustomed to mastering. It is very important that professionals who work with Hispanic families understand that immigrants might perceive the lack of English proficiency as a "disability," at least temporarily. It can also be is a huge source of mental pressure and emotional frustration that can last for several years.

Throughout their lives, adults accumulate enormous amounts of knowledge, skills, and life experiences to help them to negotiate their way through life. Conversely, if they do not master the language of the land, they do not have the means to communicate what is on their minds and hearts. Some of the adults' basic needs are independence and privacy, yet when they do not know the language, they do not have any other alternative but to depend on other people to communicate for them. As a result, not only do they lose their independence but also their privacy. They know what they want to say but do not know how to say it. By experience, I know that it feels like hundreds of pounds of water forcing its way through a small water hose. What pressure!

CHALLENGE # 2: THE MISALIGNMENT OF CULTURES

The second challenge that immigrant families are likely to face is the misalignment of cultures. Any person who immigrates to a foreign country will face the reality of a misalignment between his or her own culture and the culture of that land. As we know, culture is more than the language we speak, the food we eat, or the music to which we dance. Culture, as defined by anthropologists, is the frame of reference for people interacting with and interpreting the world in which they live. Some of the essential components of a culture are its values, beliefs, attitudes, and perceptions. The misalignment between the Hispanic immigrants' culture and the culture of the United States temporarily creates a barrier that impedes successful functioning in the new culture. What the Hispanic believes or values might not be consistent with those of the land.

CHALLENGE # 3: ADVERSE OPINIONS AND BEHAVIORS TOWARD HISPANICS

The third of the challenges that immigrant families are likely to face is adverse opinions and behaviors toward Hispanics. There are usually two reasons behind the adversity toward Hispanics. The first one is ethnocentrism, and the second is a pervasive anti-immigration sentiment.

Ethnocentric people tend to believe that one's own race or ethnicity is superior to other races and ethnicities, or that some, or all aspects of its culture, are superior to those of other groups. These people are likely to look at the world primarily from the perspective of their own culture. Ethnocentric people will not be open to people who are outside of their group, in this case Hispanics.

According to research, the anti-immigrant sentiment is not only pervasive but has also reached national levels. This sentiment has been escalating for several reasons including:

- There is a general misconception that all Hispanic immigrants are Mexicans, and that almost all Mexicans are undocumented; therefore, they should not be in this country.

- There is a high unemployment rate, and jobs are scarce; immigrants appear to be taking the few jobs that are available for the citizens of this country.

- There is an over-representation of Hispanics involved in anti-social behaviors such as drug/alcohol abuse, drug cartels, gangs, domestic violence, etc. Therefore, people in general might fear the increasing immigrant Hispanic population.

- Finally, there is a limited amount of resources for the poor, such as food stamps and non-insured medical coverage. Given the scarcity of these resources, the public in general believes that people who are legal residents of this country should be the only ones receiving these benefits.

Any Hispanic who immigrates into the United States, legally or illegally, is likely to experience some or all the adverse notions and behaviors stated above. School leaders must be aware of this reality. That way they can put in place programs to mitigate the negative impact that these misconceptions have on the Hispanic parents' ability to overcome challenges that result from immigrating into the United States.

CHALLENGE # 4: AN UNDOCUMENTED STATUS

The fourth challenge that immigrant Hispanic families are likely to face is an undocumented immigration status. There are approximately 12 million undocumented immigrants in the United States. Undocumented immigrants or "illegal aliens" are individuals who either enter the country illegally or over-stayed their visit to this country without permission. Seven million, or 59%, are Hispanics from Mexico. There are several reasons why being undocumented is a one of the greatest challenges that a significant number of Hispanic immigrants are facing today.

Undocumented immigrants cannot hold a driver's license. People who do not hold a driver licenses should not drive a car. Those who choose to drive without a license risk getting into serious trouble and possible deportation. In many places across the nation, public transportation is not always available; and even when available, it lacks the reliability needed to meet people's transportation needs.

Undocumented immigrants have a harder time finding jobs, more so than they previously did. The government is enforcing laws that prevent employers from hiring people who do not have Social Security numbers. There are systems in place for employers to ensure that the Social Security card is valid and penalties for companies that employ people without a valid Social Security card are severe.

The current higher unemployment rate is also forcing citizens and legal residents to apply for and find jobs that were usually taken by people who were undocumented. High school students often face several specific challenges. High school students who are undocumented may enroll in a Driver's Education class but cannot apply for driver's license, which affects their ability to be mobile. They cannot legally hold a part-time job, which affects their ability to support themselves and sometimes their families. They also do not qualify for Federal financial aid. Even low-income citizens, whose children qualify for Federal financial aid, have a hard time supporting their kids while they pursue a post-secondary education. What can we expect from millions of undocumented Hispanics who if they decide to pursue a post-secondary education will have to do so without a driver's license, without a part-time job and without any kind Federal financial aid?

Even undocumented students who overcome these challenges and manage to earn a post-secondary degree will have a hard time reaping the benefits of a post-secondary education. Who is going to hire an undocumented person with or without a degree?

As you can see, immigrants who are undocumented have little to none of opportunities to live the American dream. "Sin papeles" [without papers] immigrants are likely to live a life of poverty in "the shadows."

STRATEGIES TO OVERCOME CHALLENGES

After discussing some of the challenges Hispanics immigrants face, we should ask ourselves, "What strategies can we teach parents to put in place to overcome these challenges or minimize their impact upon their families?" There are five strategies that I used when I immigrated to the United States almost two decades ago. Trust me, they work! These strategies are:

- Embrace a victor versus a victim attitude;
- Seek opportunities to acquire knowledge;
- Step out of one's comfort zone; and,
- Avoid isolation at all cost.

STRATEGY # 1: EMBRACE A VICTOR VS. A VICTIM ATTITUDE

Stephen Garlington, a certified clinical social worker (LCSW) and educational consultant, believes that there are two frames of references: the "victim-ology" and the "victor-ology." People tend to use one or the other to interpret the world and react to the challenges life brings. The "victim-ology" frame of reference is propelled by a "victim" attitude. Immigrants who see the world through this lens view themselves as victims of their own circumstances. Hispanics who embrace this paradigm believe that there is little to nothing that they can do to overcome the challenges they encounter because of immigrating to a new land. The "Pobrecito yo" [poor me] attitude is alive.

On the other hand, the "victor-ology" frame of reference is propelled by a "victor" attitude. Immigrants, who see the world through this lens, see themselves as masters of their own destinies. Although they experience the same challenges, they do not view them as insurmountable. Hispanics who embrace this paradigm believe that there is a lot they can do to overcome the challenges they encounter because of immigrating to a new land.

For Hispanic immigrants to achieve a quality life, they will need to embrace the "victor-ology" life paradigm. The "Si puedo" [Yes, I can] attitude needs to be alive. Parents who have a "victor-ology" attitude will likely be open and motivated to implement strategies that could help them overcome their personal challenges.

STRATEGY # 2: SEEK OPPORTUNITIES TO ACQUIRE KNOWLEDGE

The second strategy I propose is to seek opportunities to acquire knowledge. Someone once said, "Knowledge is power." On the other hand, according to the Old Testament prophet Hosea, the lack of knowledge can bring destruction to an entire population. Hispanic parents must understand the importance of setting aside time to learn. We must teach them that it is imperative that they enroll in programs and participate in activities in which they can:

- Increase their level of English proficiency;
- Increase their level of education;

- Acquire a deeper understanding of the American culture;

- Learn how to use the different technological devices that are available for the general public; and,

- Learn about laws that have a direct or indirect impact on the immigrant population, documented and undocumented.

Many Hispanics who immigrate to the United States end up working in jobs that pay very little and might not require specific skills, despite their having had careers back in their countries. This is most likely due to their lack of language skills to practice their careers here in the United States. It does not matter how educated or experienced people are; if they are not competent in the language of the land, they will end up in jobs that will not reward knowledge or expertise. Hispanic parents must move up the ladder of language acquisition, from the silent stage to proficiency.

Allow me to share a personal story to illustrate my point. Dr. Darlene Ruscitti, Regional Superintendent of Schools of the DuPage Regional Office of Education, asked me to gather more information about the Hispanic man who came every evening to clean her office.

"He is so different from any other custodian that I have met," she said. "He behaves like a very educated man."

I immediately looked for him the next day and, after a brief, but very interesting conversation, I learned that he had a degree in Psychology and another degree in Theology. He was a priest assistant back in Peru.

"This is all I can do for now because I can hardly speak English," he said. With a lot of conviction, I responded, "This is all you will ever do if you don't go to school to learn English."

Without English competency, immigrants cannot reach their potential in this country. That is a fact. After several brief conversations during encounters in the halls of the building where we both worked, I convinced him to enroll in the English as a Second Language (ESL) program at the College of DuPage. I made the call myself and got him to speak to the bilingual ESL program assistant. Today, he goes to school religiously! His self-esteem and confidence have sky-rocketed. As a result, he became motivated enough to submit the necessary documents to have his degree validated in the United States. He is also volunteering time assisting the priest of a Catholic church with a large number of Hispanic parishioners. I am sure you agree with me that English competency is the gateway for immigrants to reach their potential.

STRATEGY # 3: STEP OUT OF THEIR COMFORT ZONE

The third strategy that I strongly recommend is to step out of their comfort zone. It is so hard to move out of the zone in which we are comfortable, right? Every time I go to church, I always sit in the same seat. I feel like I own that seat; I feel like I belong. People give up the comfort of belonging by leaving homelands. All the people who come to this country must move out of their comfort zones in order to move up the ladder of acculturation.

It does not take long before the immigrant emerges from the "honeymoon" or fascination stage of acculturation and experiences hostility or frustration for not understanding or sharing the culture of the new land. Immigrants must adjust as soon as possible and then move up to biculturalism, which is the ability to navigate both Hispanic and the American mainstream cultures.

However, the basic truth is that immigrants are not going to learn the American mainstream culture staying home, watching only Hispanic television channels, listening only to Hispanic radio stations, attending only the Spanish church services, or just relating to people who are Hispanics. The only way to understand the American culture (what they believe, what they value, how they interact with each other, how they interpret the world and life experiences) is by "hanging out" with Americans. It is intimidating, especially for the newly arrived immigrants, but it must be done.

I usually share with the parents during my Hispanic Parent workshops that one of the tactics that helped me increase my level of acculturation and English proficiency was to attend an English-speaking church. Before that, I only attended services in Spanish. I felt out of place for a few months. I was not able to understand the entire sermon, and I could not understand nor pronounce the lyrics of the worship songs (and I love to sing). Nevertheless, I was determined. The services started and finished on time (all the time) and lasted an hour and a half, instead of three hours, like the services I was accustomed to. Americans seem to always be very time-conscious.

While attending this English-speaking church, I also learned to give people more space when conversing and to not to be so overly affectionate. I mean, I did not have to kiss or hug every member I encountered. I simply smiled or offered a handshake. I can testify today that by stepping out of my comfort zone and attending a non-Hispanic church, I learned about the mainstream American culture and increased my English language skills like never before that time. Stepping out of my comfort zone paid great dividends.

STRATEGY # 4: AVOID ISOLATION AT ALL COST

The fourth and last of the strategies that I propose is to avoid isolation at all cost. The challenges that immigrant families face are too immense. Immigrants cannot and should not face those challenges alone. We must teach Hispanic parents that they must establish positive and productive connections with the right people and then stay connected. Who are these "right people?"

These "right people" are what we call "Cultural Informants." Cultural Informants are caring and trusting individuals who have a very good understanding of the immigration phenomena. They could be school parent-liaisons, social workers, teachers, community leaders, etc. who have the knowledge and skills needed to help immigrant families overcome their challenges. Cultural Informants, in the context of a Hispanic parental involvement program, must be able to provide opportunities in which the immigrant parents can discuss their precarious situations. Cultural Informants can provide immigrants with coping skills for dealing with typical feelings such as hopelessness, isolation-dislocation, fear, anxiety, etc. Organizations that want to implement successful Hispanic parental involvement programs must include cultural informant roles. The kind of support these informants provide immigrant families will be a key determinant factor in the level of success immigrant parents will experience in the United States.

Most Hispanics immigrate into the United States voluntarily; they are here because they want to be here. Period! But the reality is that once they are here, they are likely to face challenges beyond the imagination of people who have not gone through the immigration experience. I strongly believe that educators must provide parents with strategies to help them overcome, or at least minimize, the impact of these challenges. The spirit of an immigrant is the spirit of an eagle. Let's teach them how to use the winds of adversity to overcome their challenges. If we do that, parents will be in a better position to parent their children and support their academic development. You and I know that parental involvement will definitely improve children's academic achievement. In the end, that is what we all want.

CHAPTER 4

COMPETENCY # 4: MAINTAIN FAMILY UNITY

Parents reduce potential family divisions due to linguistic, cultural, educational, digital, and immigration-status gaps.

"Their kids (Hispanics) have a harder time because, well, they can't go home and get help from their parents since they probably know more than their parents. Most of their parents don't even know English which could be hard if you have an English project or something. They need to focus in school and realize that if they don't do what they have to do they're going to struggle in life as adults and Whites or others will keep on discriminating against us and keep putting us down. But we can change that and prove them wrong because we all have the same education at school so nothing really makes us different from them." - Pablo, Hispanic High School Student

COMPETENCY # 4: MAINTAIN FAMILY UNITY

In the Latino community, the family is the most important source and transmitter of Hispanic culture. As a Hispanic, I know that we value family the way that individuals from the mainstream culture of the United States value freedom. Family is extremely important in the Hispanic community. Nevertheless, the integrity of the immigrant Hispanic family is threatened by the family-divide.

GAPS THAT CAUSE THE FAMILY DIVIDE

The family-divide is a term that I use to describe a chasm caused by linguistic, cultural, digital, educational, and immigration-status gaps, which are formed between the family members when school-aged children of Hispanic families enroll in the American educational system. These  gaps can cause a family-divide the same way that cracks in the foundation can bring a building down. I believe that the ability to close or minimize these gaps is one of the competencies Hispanic parents must demonstrate.

GAP # 1: LINGUISTIC

Educators observe and bring about the progress of Hispanic children moving from one level of language acquisition to the next higher level - from the "silent" to the proficient level. While this is happening, the parents' proficiency in English remains the same, creating a linguistic gap. The linguistic gap can adversely affect the family dynamics. It is my opinion that this gap is the one that most seriously causes a divide in a family.

The linguistic gap adversely affects the parent-child communication process. In school, kids start "losing" their Spanish and eventually may not have enough Spanish proficiency to comfortably express thoughts and feelings in their parents' language. I have personally experienced this with Deborah, my youngest daughter.

During her middle and high school years, I remember saying to her again and again, "Baby, please talk to me in Spanish! It is hard for me to speak English at home. It feels like I am still working."

I usually got a "Olvídalo mami" response, which meant, "Forget it, mom." That was usually the end of the conversation for that evening.

The linguistic gap can also lead to "role-reversal." By role-reversal I mean that the parent in some way becomes dependent upon the child with the child now playing a parental role. Many times Hispanic children become part-time interpreters, translators, and cultural brokers. They translate all kinds of written documents that are sent to their parents. They are their parents' interpreters in many situations such as meeting with the immigration lawyer, pleading a traffic citation in court, attending a parent- teacher conference, and even accompanying in a doctor's visit. I learned, not too long ago, about a sixth grade child who missed school to interpret for his mom during a doctor's appointment, letting his mom know for the first time that she had cancer. I am sure that you will agree with me that children do not have the level of maturity needed to be exposed to or deal with information that is directed to adults.

The linguistic gap may also impede parents from becoming involved in their children's education in the way that schools need parents to be involved. In too many cases, students are the ones who inform their parents about what is going on in school. Sometimes the information that parents receive through their children is either distorted, inaccurate, or does not even get to them at all.

For example, during one of my "Student Institute Day" seminars, a Latino student said, "I prefer not to give my parents all those papers that the school sends home. It is hard for me because I have to translate everything. It takes a lot of time! Many times I do not have the time to do that or do not know the right words in Spanish. I mean, I do understand what my parents are saying, but I can't speak Spanish that well."

GAP # 2: CULTURAL

The second gap that threatens to divide the Hispanic family is the cultural gap. As Hispanic children's grade-levels increase, they also ascend to higher levels of acculturation. They go from the "honeymoon" to the acculturation level. In contrast, their parents' acculturation levels appear to be stationary. The cultural gap produces dysfunctional family dynamics because it produces generational misalignment of values, beliefs, attitudes, and perceptions. The children's perceptions about themselves and the world around them begin to differ from their parents' perceptions as they mature.

I experienced this cultural gap within my own family when my youngest, Deborah, expressed her desire to pursue a Visual Arts career at Cooper Union in Manhattan, New York. We were living in West Palm Beach. I was a single mom, and she was the only child left at home; my other two children had already left the nest. I thought, "How in the world would she dare to contemplate a thought like that!"

You see, my other two kids, who were mostly raised in Guatemala, didn't leave home until they married or finished college. They both attended a nearby university. They both had excellent grades and lots of opportunities, but staying together as a family was more important than pursuing individual goals and desires. But this "little one" was different. She had her personal aspirations and saw herself as more of an individual than as part of a collective family. I had to adjust to her leaving to pursue her own path.

GAP # 3: DIGITAL

The digital gap occurs when children enroll in school and are exposed to a great variety of new technologies. Most school curriculums across the nation include content with technology components. At an early age, kids achieve mastery over technological innovations while their parents' technological proficiency is virtually non-existent. While the digital divide may occur in mainstream families as well, it is widened by language and cultural divides in Hispanic families.

The digital divide creates a disadvantage in the parents' ability to supervise their children's exposure to inappropriate content and stimuli. We parents usually spend a significant amount of our time and energy trying to protect our children from all kinds of dangers that threaten their physical, emotional, and social well-being. But, when kids have access to a computer at home, in many ways it is like a Trojan Horse. It looks so innocent on the outside, but it has the potential to undermine parents' efforts to protect their children from social ills, such as pornography, on-line predators, bullies, etc. Kids can visit forbidden websites or communicate with undesirable people without their parents' knowledge. Hispanic parents may not have the skills to supervise how their children are using technology.

In one of my focus group conversations with Latino high school students, one student said, "My parents don't know, and they do not know how to know."

Parents' lack of computer skills prevents them from searching the web, accessing the school website, or using electronic mail. Parents have a diminished ability to communicate with the teachers and the school, and vice versa. More than ever before, schools are building websites to provide the public all kinds of information about the school. These parents also have a diminished access to their children's grades and scores on tests and assignments. Teachers and parents can connect through email, but what good does that do when so many of our Latino parents don't even know how to turn on a computer?

GAP # 4: EDUCATIONAL

The educational gap is formed when children enroll in our educational system and sometimes make progress beyond the educational level of their parents. It is very difficult for parents to monitor or supervise their children's educational progress when they have a lower level of education.

This educational gap is very different from a language gap. When parents have a strong educational background, in whatever language, they are more likely to have a good understanding based on their own experience of "what it takes" to master an academic content, cognitively, emotionally, and socially. I guarantee you that these parents will be behind their kids' academic careers in spite of their language limitations. They will find ways to connect with the school and the teachers! But parents who have not experienced academic success themselves might not be able to coach their children's academic careers. Imagine having an athletic coach who has never played the sport himself.

The educational gap may manifest itself in another way. Some parents, who struggled in school when they were young, may have the tendency to justify their children's lack of success in school.

I hear many parents say again and again, "I also had a lot of trouble in school when I was a child; that is why I only finished elementary (school)."

They may have the desire to see their kids be "alguien importante en la vida" [Be someone important in life], but, in reality, they do not expect them to achieve. Someone once said that "there is a long way between a desire and an expectation." Parents who have not experienced academic success might also feel very satisfied if their kids just graduate from high school.

For example, one Hispanic high school student once said to me, "My parents are more than happy if I just graduate high school because I will be the first one in the family to graduate. So, they just expect me to pass my classes. I do not have to earn A's and B's or pass any of those tests people take to go to college, the ACT or whatever."

The educational gap can also challenge the parent-child relationship in which parents are the authority and children are subordinate to that authority. There is a lot of upward mobility in American society. Education can open the doors to great opportunities. Children very soon learn that a college degree can not only provide a greater income, but also cultivate respect and sometimes prestige. Although the outcome is not always realized, students might forget that, in spite of their parents' low level of education, their parents made huge sacrifices. They left their countries and everything known to them in order to provide their children an opportunity for a better future. Sometimes when the children reach those teenage years, they might feel embarrassed because of their parents. They may not want their teachers or peers to know their parents.

I remember a phone conversation with a very caring high school mathematics teacher. I was trying to help her understand some facts about Hispanic students. She shared with me that it was very hard for her to communicate with one of her student's parents.

She said to me. "I send notes home with Carlos and never get a response," and then she added: "I have even called home several times. Carlos always took the calls and said that his parents were not there. I then realized that Carlos did not want me to talk to his parents and definitely not to meet them in person. Through our parent liaison, a wonderful Hispanic man, I finally got hold of his mother and met both Carlos' father and mother in a parent-teacher conference to discuss Carlos' curricular program for the next year. During that meeting, Carlos acted so weird. He didn't look at me and didn't look at his parents. He acted like he was embarrassed by his family. What a shame! His parents had a humble appearance and could not speak English. But I am telling you, he had the most loving parents in the world."

GAP # 5: IMMIGRATION-STATUS

Any family divide is amplified when Latino children are born in the U.S. to parents who are undocumented, creating a split or a gap in their immigration status. This immigration-status gap presents enormous challenges that are hard for many of us to even imagine.

These students experience a great deal of fear and anxiety regarding the possibility that their parents might be deported without warning or preparation, leading to a family's emotional, social, and financial crisis. In one of my trips to North Carolina, I visited different classrooms at the elementary, middle, and high school levels. I wanted to have a better understanding of their state's education system. I was also in search of some insights about the challenges that Latinos students were facing in that specific state. To engage students in a group conversation, I asked a group of third graders the following question: "If I was your "Madrina" [Godmother] and I had all the power in the world, what would you ask me to do?" One cute little boy raised his hand really high to get my attention.

I said to him, "Yes, my dear, what would you ask me to do?" I was shocked with his response.

While speaking in a soft manner and a sad tone, he said, "Can you make deportation stop?"

To tell you the truth, I did not know how to respond. The teacher later explained to me that there were many students at that school that were worried that their parents would be taken away by

Immigration and Custom Enforcement (ICE), while they were in school and they would find themselves "home alone."

Another issue is that parents who are undocumented, even if their children are citizens, avoid communicating with teachers or the schools, or participating in school events due to the fear of being "outed." It creates a sense of isolation or "living in the shadows."

Sometimes teachers and school administrators are very disappointed with the small numbers of parents that show up in any kind of school event or program, especially when they have provided interpretation in Spanish and have targeted the parents of their English Language Learner (ELL) students. This phenomenon frequently happens in schools that are located in areas with significant numbers of undocumented parents. Participation tends to be poor unless the school staff has been successful in establishing a connection with the community and gaining their trust.

Not long ago, I was the keynote speaker at a Hispanic Parent Night in a small city in Illinois, a city that had a 50% Hispanic population. One of the parents who attended my presentation came to me at the end and said, "I came in spite that some of my friends and relatives advised me not to. ICE has been here in these past weeks and deported many people. There are parents who thought ICE would be here today because there are so many of us in one single place. We came, but we are all leaving through different doors in case they come."

I strongly believe that these five gaps threaten to divide the Hispanic family and are likely to have a significant adverse impact in the dynamics of the Latino family nucleus. Like cracks, these gaps can seriously damage the foundation of the family structure.

STRATEGIES TO MINIMIZE THE FAMILY-DIVIDE GAPS

I believe that these gaps can lead to parental disempowerment and hinder parents' ability to advocate for their children's academic success. How can we help Hispanic parents eliminate or at least reduce these gaps? There are five proven-to-work strategies that educators can use to help Hispanic parents. These strategies are:

1. Increase their level of English proficiency;
2. Develop a better understanding of the USA mainstream culture;
3. Increase their level of digital literacy;
4. Increase their level of education; and,
5. Increase their understanding of immigrant-related laws and prepare for possible sudden separation.

STRATEGY # 1: INCREASE THEIR LEVEL OF ENGLISH PROFICIENCY

Educators need to encourage parents to increase their level of English proficiency. Increasing competency in the English language is not an option. It is difficult for an immigrant family to pursue a quality life in the United States without a certain level of English proficiency. How can they do that? They have to enroll in any English as a Second Language (ESL) adult program so they can move up the ladder of language acquisition in a structured manner. No matter how busy they are, or how hard they work, increasing their English language skills must be at the top of their priorities.

The process of language acquisition can be accelerated when parents participate in activities in which people communicate primarily in the English language. We can encourage parents to attend or participate in English-speaking religious services of their choice, even just four times a month. These services are usually short - less than two hours. They can also watch the news in English, one hour a day, local or national. They can also be encouraged to listen to the radio in English while they are going and coming back from work. It is very difficult to develop English language skills when all you are exposed to all day is Spanish. Don't you think? I always tell parents: "The same way that a car without gas cannot take you where you need to be. Hard work alone, without language skills, will not allow you to reach the American dream. English is the gas!

STRATEGY # 2: DEVELOP A BETTER UNDERSTANDING OF THE USA MAINSTREAM CULTURE

We must help parents develop the ability to participate in

mainstream American culture. This starts with understanding it, but it does not happen in a day. It is a slow process that can take years. Parents can learn a lot about the mainstream American culture through reading. There are an enormous amount of books, articles, and websites dedicated to do just this. But, that requires a level of English language skills that immigrant parents might not have. So, another way that parents can learn more about the mainstream culture of this country is by participating in events and activities in which they have ample opportunities to observe and interact with people from the mainstream culture. Interacting with the educational system is a place to start.

Many of the Hispanic families that I have known throughout these years live in communities with a high percent of Hispanic people. They watch Hispanic channels, listen to Hispanic radio stations, shop in Hispanic stores, and attend church services in Spanish. They can pretty much go about their lives with minimal interaction with people outside of the Hispanic community. Parents are often too comfortable interacting only with people of their own ethnicity and who speak their language. They must learn to step out of this comfort zone!

Parents can also learn about the culture (and also improve their English language skills) by watching television shows or movies. In my opinion, it is an avenue to observe how mainstream American people, within a specific context, behave and interact with each other. Parents can listen to different English radio stations to have a better understanding of the different musical genres such as rock, country, jazz, etc. Parents can attend school and community events well attended by native-English speakers.

I mentioned before about attending English-speaking religious services. This particular strategy worked for me. I came into the United States in 1990 and established myself in Dade County, Florida. As you know, South Florida is an area heavily populated by Hispanics, especially Cubans. You hear and speak Spanish almost everywhere, and this significantly slowed down my acquisition of English. It was not until I moved to Palm Beach County that I became immersed in the American mainstream culture. English was spoken everywhere! I got heavy exposure and ample opportunities to practice my English language skills. In 1997, for the first time, I attended a large English-speaking church. At that time, almost 100% of their membership was Caucasian. What a cultural shock! I soon learned through observation that I was not supposed to be kissing and hugging everyone I met.

You see, for many Latinos, a small conversation can be perceived as the beginning of a new relationship. Once you feel you know somebody, you are likely to greet that person with affection such as a hug, a kiss on the cheek, or both. Since I realized that I was a "hugger" and a "kisser," to aid me in refraining, I wrote on a paper "¡No beses a nadie!" That means, "Do not kiss anybody!" I attached that paper on my wrist every Sunday for the next several weeks. I reminded myself to just smile, say "hi," or shake hands. The years that I attended that church not only improved my English language skills significantly, but also allowed me to develop a better understanding of what it meant to be part of the American mainstream culture. I learned a lot through observation and interactions about how to behave and interact with people out of my own ethnic community.

STRATEGY # 3: INCREASE THEIR LEVEL OF DIGITAL LITERACY

Another very important strategy to reduce potential family divisions is to encourage parents to acquire knowledge and skills related to the use of computers and other technologies so they can bridge the digital gap that I talked about earlier in this chapter. Parents need to become aware of the importance and advantages of becoming computer literate. They need to gain confidence that computer literacy is something they can obtain. Many of the schools that offer ESL courses also offer courses that teach adults how to use computers and many of the most popular kinds of software. Through these courses, parents can learn, among many other skills, how to "surf the web," how to get into different websites and obtain information, and how to send and receive emails. These are all skills that will help parents interact with the school system.

STRATEGY # 4: INCREASE THEIR LEVEL OF EDUCATION

Another proven-to-work strategy that can help immigrant Hispanic parents reduce or close the educational gap, which could exist within their families, is to return to school. Parents must actively seek to improve their educational levels. If they never finished school back in their native countries, they can enroll in a General Educational Development (GED) program. Parents with low levels of English proficiency have the option to enroll in a GED program in Spanish. I have a friend, Hugo Montalvo, who is doing exactly that right now. His self-esteem used to be low, which affected his level of self-confidence. Since he enrolled in the Spanish GED program, he became aware of the many opportunities that are waiting for him. He now has dreams and goals! This program is boosting his self-esteem and confidence. There is a saying in Latin America that states, "¡Nunca es tarde cuando la dicha es buena!" Roughly translated, it means that "it is never too late when there is still an opportunity."

Immigrant parents who have already completed their secondary education must be encouraged to pursue post-secondary education. Right now, a high school diploma alone does not guarantee a job that pays sufficiently or provides additional fringe benefits. Two and four-year programs are not the only options. It can be a six-month educational or vocational program. What matters is that they learn a specialty or trade that is in high demand.

Not long ago, I met a Hispanic family. The parents were in their thirties and had kids enrolled in an elementary school in which I was facilitating a parent workshop. When I was done with the presentation and opened the floor for questions or concerns, a couple asked me for permission to share some words with the audience. The father and the mother stood straight and with their heads high - a kind of body language that indicated self-confidence. The father testified how much he had suffered working at a place that not only did not pay well, but did not give him any job satisfaction. He could hardly speak English.

He enrolled in school to learn English. After that, he enrolled in a program that certified him as a Heating and Air Conditioning Technician. He said to all of us, "People used to make fun of me. But nobody makes fun of me now. I now feel proud of what I do, and I am more able to provide for my family."

STRATEGY # 5: INCREASE THEIR UNDERSTANDING OF IMMIGRANT-RELATED LAWS AND PREPARE FOR POSSIBLE SUDDEN SEPARATION

This last strategy only applies to parents who have an immigration-status gap in their families; that is, they are undocumented, and their children were born here in the United States. I do not know if, by the time you are reading this, the situation of millions of undocumented Hispanic families has changed in this country. The undocumented sector of the Hispanic population not only lives in constant fear of being deported, but also has little chance finding jobs, any jobs. They are waiting, hoping that in the midst of the current financial crisis and anti-immigrant sentiment that some kind of law or comprehensive immigration reform could allow them to become legal residents and avoid deportation. Legal residency will open the doors for more job opportunities, which could improve the quality of their lives. Meanwhile, what can undocumented Hispanic parents do?

We must communicate to Hispanic immigrant parents that they should not "freeze" or put everything on hold. On the contrary, they must spend their time and mental and emotional energy growing in all aspects of their lives. If sudden deportation comes, they will be better prepared to pursue an improved life back in their countries, or in any other country in the world where they might end up living.

Parents must increase their level of English proficiency. The English language skills that they learn will help them here in the United States. It will also be their greatest asset if they go back to their homelands. They must strategize to develop a better understanding of the mainstream American culture. Knowledge is power! Bilingualism and biculturalism opens doors here and in any part of the world. They must become computer literate. Computer skills are needed here as well as in any part of the world. Last but not least, they must increase their level of education. Earn a GED diploma if they have never completed high school or a post-secondary career. If they learn to reduce the potential gaps here, it will help them in their countries of origin. Knowledge really is power. Personal growth and knowledge is theirs to keep wherever they are.

The family divide caused by linguistic, cultural, digital, educational, and sometimes immigration status gaps threatens the integrity of the Hispanic family. We must create awareness among Hispanic parents of this threat and ask them to take an active role in minimizing the gaps. There is no way around this issue. Parents must learn the language of the land, English. They need to develop a better understanding of the culture in which their kids are being raised, the American mainstream culture. Parents need to do whatever it takes to increase their level of education and technological skills. And, if they don't have "papeles" [legal status residency], they must learn and grow in all aspect of their lives. That way if sudden deportation comes, they will be better prepared to improve the quality of their lives back in their native countries. Closing or minimizing these five gaps will empower parents to support their children's academic development. Increasing parental involvement leads to increased student academic achievement. In the end, this is what we educators want.

CHAPTER 5

COMPETENCY # 5: UNDERSTAND THEIR ROLE

Parents understand the role that they need to play in their children's education.

"One thing with the whole parent issue is that maybe parents can be given some understanding of our education. My parents don't understand the school system and they don't know how to know. Schools should teach our parents how to help us in any way they can because their help can make a big impact in our lives. You know, in many cases they are our biggest influence in life." - Jorge, Hispanic High School Student

COMPETENCY # 5: UNDERSTAND THEIR ROLE

After more than thirty years of experience as a mother, teacher, school administrator, and consultant in education, I am convinced that our public educational system functions at its best when parents are part of their children's academic lives. In my opinion, this is why parents' capability to embrace and play their roles must be a competency that Hispanic parents develop.

THE VALUE OF EDUCATION

I have long learned that the United States places great value on education because it considers itself the great equalizer of democratic society. Horace Mann is quoted as saying, "Education then, beyond all other devices of human origin, is the great equalizer of the conditions of men, the balance wheel of the social machinery." People who reach higher levels of education are more likely to transition to the mainstream middle class. It is common knowledge that the middle class is the engine of economic stability and the backbone of our democratic political structure. Countries with citizens who are disproportionately living in poverty are more likely to experience economic and political turmoil. Educating all children is a matter of political, economic, and social stability.

HISPANIC ACADEMIC ACHIEVEMENT

During Hispanic workshops and community events, I always try to share with the audience facts and statistics that can increase their awareness of the current situation of the Hispanic community in the United States. Hispanics are the largest minority and the fastest growing ethnicity in the United States. According to the USA Census, Hispanics grew from almost 15 million in the 1980's to 50.5 million in our decade. They are now 16.3% of the total USA population. The Hispanic population also accounted for most of the nation's growth, 56% from 2000 to 2010; however, 67% live in poverty. A high poverty rate has been linked to a low level of educational attainment.

Parents must be informed that by the age of nine, when students are likely to be in fourth grade, Hispanic students are two grade levels behind the average White or Asian child. Hispanic students have lower standardized test scores than their White and Asian peers in mathematics, reading, and science. Only 57% of Hispanic students graduate from high school and barely 10% earn a college degree. Hispanics are the most undereducated group of the youth cohort in the U.S. population. The collision of increasing numbers of Hispanics in our nation with their corresponding low educational attainment is likely to produce a national disaster. That is why I believe that helping Hispanics to achieve greater academic success is a matter of national security!

IMPROVING PARENTAL INVOLVEMENT IMPROVES ACADEMIC ACHIEVEMENT

What can we do to help Hispanic students achieve greater academic success so they are in a stronger position to move into the American middle class? There are numerous strategies that educational leaders have implemented. The government is currently holding teachers more accountable for all their students' performance on state accountability tests hoping that this will improve classroom instruction. Some school districts are offering financial incentives to attract the best teachers to instruct at schools with high percentages of minority and low income students. States across the nation are investing in contemporary books and instructional materials while their curriculums are being revised and aligned to the states' standards and assessments. Standardized tests are being revised and new ones are being purchased hoping that better assessment systems could lead to improved student performance. But what about increasing parental involvement?

Research in many studies indicates that parental involvement is one of the leading indicators of student academic achievement. As educators, you know that when parents are involved, there is improved student academic achievement, better school attendance, better classroom discipline, reduced dropout rates, greater student self-esteem and self-confidence, and greater conduciveness to learning school culture. The improvements that parental involvement brings occur regardless of the economic, racial, or cultural background of the families. Parental involvement makes a significant difference in the quality of education that students will experience. This holds true for Hispanic students.

THE AMERICAN EDUCATIONAL SYSTEM – A TRICYCLE

I use the metaphor of a tricycle to explain the American educational system in the Hispanic parent trainings that I do. The same way that a tricycle needs three wheels to function properly, the student, the teacher, and the parent need to collaborate to reach the academic outcome of a quality education. The front wheel of the tricycle, which is the largest, represents the student. The same way that the front wheel  determines the direction of the tricycle, the students' needs determine the course of action to help them reach academic proficiency in their academic subjects.

The two back wheels of the tricycle represent the teacher and the parent. Teachers play an essential role in a child's academic development. In school, teachers create the right classroom environment, facilitate and lead the kinds of activities and experiences that children need to learn. The teacher-student learning occurs during school hours, which is only a fraction of a student's daily life. We know that education does not end when the kids leave school.

That is where parents must responsibly accept their role in their children's total educational development. The parents are represented by the second back wheel of the tricycle. They must also create the right home environment and support the kinds of educational experiences that would allow their children to continue learning to reach proficiency in all academic subjects.

Neither the teacher nor the parent does it alone. A tricycle's two back wheels are attached to each other to provide support and balance. Parents and teachers must work collaboratively to provide students the kind of support and balance they need to reach their maximum potential and contribute to society. Hispanic parents must be aware that the role they play in their children's education is as important as the teachers' role. If we do the math, during a year's time, students will spend more time at home than in school. What kind of involvement should be expected from our Hispanic parents?

DEFINING HISPANIC PARENTAL INVOLVEMENT

There are several traditional ways that parents become involved in their children's education. Examples include:

- Assuming leadership roles in their children's schools by sitting on councils or committees and participating in their children's schools decision-making processes.

- Helping or providing assistance by volunteering time as teachers' aides, schools' tutors, chaperones, etc. at their children's schools.

- Organizing fundraising events or soliciting financial contributions for their children's schools.

- Participating in the formal activities, events, or meetings of their children's schools.

- Improving the academic achievement of their children by initiating at home learning activities, tutoring, and helping with projects or homework.

Can we realistically expect all immigrant parents to get involved in a significant way in the examples above? While not all Hispanic parents are overwhelmed with the challenges that most immigrants face, some may still lack the knowledge and skills needed to participate in school committees, work as school volunteers and so forth. We need to ask ourselves, "What kind of involvement do we need the most and what kind can we realistically expect to get from Hispanic parents?"

I have been an educational consultant and researcher for the past five years. I have asked hundreds of teachers who work in schools with high percentages of Hispanic students, "What do you need your students' parents to do at home to support what you do in school? What can your students' parents do to help you get more Hispanic students to reach proficiency in reading and mathematics?"

I was surprised to learn that teachers were not concerned about parents' lack of participation in school committees or fundraising events. They did not need or expect Hispanic parents to work as school volunteers or to tutor their children at home. The teachers that I interviewed consistently expressed that they needed open two-way communications with the Hispanic parents. They required parents to put in place home strategies that ensure homework completion. They wanted parents to encourage their children to practice daily reading at home to help their children reach higher levels of reading proficiency. Most of all, they long for Hispanic parents to teach their children the character traits that are conducive to academic success such as responsibility, persistence, a smart-hard work ethic, and the ability to delay gratification. I have spoken to thousands of Hispanic parents from Los Angeles to Chicago to Florida explaining the tricycle and teaching the specifics of what to do to get involved in the ways teachers needed them to be involved. The specifics that I teach about such as connecting with teachers, supervising homework, practicing reading at home, and developing character are discussed in detail in Chapters 7 – 10.

As educators, we must be clear in reference to what we need and expect our Hispanic parents to do in spite of the challenges they might be facing or their lack of knowledge and skills. Schools can implement programs to teach Hispanic parents and empower them to succeed in their role and responsibility of supporting their kids' achievement of a quality education.

By experience, I know that parents are more motivated and willing to assume the role of the "third wheel of the tricycle" if they become aware of the Hispanic lack of academic achievement and low performance in their states' accountability tests at the local, state and national levels. I have witnessed how this awareness creates a sense of urgency that can lead to increased involvement.

Not long ago I conducted a series of parent workshops in one of the suburban school districts in the state of Illinois. Six of the seven schools within the district were in school improvement status for not meeting the NCLB state goals. Seventy percent of the student population was Hispanic. During the workshops, I shared with the Hispanic community the performance of the students in the state's accountability test, Illinois State Assessment Test (ISAT), at the state, district and school levels. The schools' administrators and I hand-delivered and explained their children's individual test results. The purpose of doing this was to increase parental involvement by helping them understand the impact of their children's scores on the schools' and the district's school improvement status and their children's academic future. These kinds of parent workshops not only inform, but also create the sense of urgency needed to get parents involved the way that teachers need them to be involved. I know that most Hispanic parents are not aware or don't understand the NCLB law, the purpose and use of the state's accountability tests, and how to read and interpret their children's individual ISAT reports.

I also know that Hispanic parents are more inspired to assume the responsibilities of their role if they embrace the idea that a quality education leads to a quality life. We must realize that many Latino parents come from countries where this is not necessarily true. Where they are from, education does not necessarily open doors to an improved life style. Who their parents are, or what their families' financial resources are, plays a much larger role in determining what doors are open for them. In Chapter One, I provided a more detailed discussion about embracing the idea that a quality education in America leads to a quality life, the first of the ten parent competencies presented in this book.

We must also help our Hispanic parents believe in their children's potential to learn. Parents who believe in their children's ability to learn are more likely to become involved in their academic lives. Also, parents who believe in their children's potential to learn are able to protect them from negative beliefs, attitudes, and perceptions that could cause their kids to internalize an idea that they do not have what it takes to achieve academic success. When parents have this belief, they can sometimes transmit it to their children. When parents believe in their children, sooner or later children will believe in themselves. Believing in their children's ability to learn is one of the ten competencies we must help parents reach. This competency is discussed in detail in the following chapter.

When parents understand how the American education system works and the responsibilities that their role entails, they are more likely to step up and take the necessary steps to get involved in their children's education the way that teachers need them to be involved. This involvement includes connecting and collaborating with their children's teachers, supervising homework completion, making reading a family habit, and teaching their children the character traits that lead to academic and life success. Parents must understand that the school system needs their involvement the same way that the tricycle needs that back wheel.

I know for a fact that Hispanic parents are more motivated and willing to play their role when they are aware of the current continuing achievement gaps between Hispanic students and their White and Asian peers; embrace the idea that a quality education leads to a quality life; and learn to believe in their children's potential to learn and expect them to achieve. The role of the parent in a child's academic development is absolutely vital.

CHAPTER 6

COMPETENCY # 6: BELIEVE IN THEIR CHILDREN

Parents believe, expect, and understand how their children can learn.

"It has to do a lot with the parents. White students' parents have a lot to do with their students' education. They care a lot about their grades. In my case my parents are satisfied if I get a C, as long as I pass the class. Hispanic parents care, but not that much. They don't expect their kids to try as hard as they should. Most Hispanic parents have lower expectations. White parents make their children work harder; they want the best. They are not satisfied with a C." - Enrique, Hispanic High School Student

COMPETENCY # 6: BELIEVE IN THEIR CHILDREN

One competency that every Hispanic parent must have is to believe, expect and know how their children can learn. What do I mean by this? The same way that a small plant needs soil, water and light to grow, children will need their parents to believe in their ability to learn, expect them to succeed in school, and, understand the essential elements involved in the process of reaching proficiency in any academic subject.

PARENTS BELIEVE IN THEIR CHILDREN'S ABILITY TO LEARN

Through parent workshops, parent-teacher conferences, or any kind of encounters teachers have with parents, teachers can help parents to believe in their children's academic potentials. Parents who believe in their children's ability to learn are more likely to become involved in their academic lives. Also, parents who believe in their children's potential to learn are able to protect their children from negative forces that could cause them to internalize the idea that they do not have what it takes to achieve academic success. When parents believe in their children, sooner or later children will learn to believe in themselves.

In my many years of experience as a high school mathematics

teacher, I saw a significant number of students who were convinced they did not have the ability or the "genes" to pass my mathematics class. Their attitudes toward math were so negative that they did not participate in class, do homework, or study for the tests. They set themselves up for failure. But what concerned me the most was that their parents did not believe in their children's ability either and therefore did not expect them to do well in my class. This lack of belief was manifested in a parent-teacher conference I once had with the father of a student who was struggling in my class. This parent said to me: "My son is not good in mathematics. He does not have the brains to do well in math. He is like me. I hated math when I was in school. I will be happy if he just passes the class this year, so he does not have to repeat it again next year. However, I really appreciate your interest in helping my son."

It is very difficult, if not impossible, for teachers to get parents involved in their children's education if parents don't believe their children have the ability to excel in school. Their beliefs fuel their actions and inactions. Parents are less likely to make reading a habit, monitor their children's homework, and establish connections with their children's teachers if they do not think their involvement can make a difference. If their children do not have the potential to learn, why should they bother?

There are many outside negative forces that constantly threaten students' capability to believe in their ability to learn. Parents must be aware of these forces so they can minimize, or eliminate, the negative impact that these elements can have on their children's academic careers. But, parents can only do that if they believe in their children's potential. One of these forces is the Innate Ability theory. People who embrace this theory judge that innate ability alone determines what and how much students can learn; it will determine the level of academic success that children will experience in school. People who support this theory believe that some people "have it" and some do not; that is, some people can learn and some cannot. When students believe that they are "one of those" who simply do not "have it," why would they bother to get involved in activities that could improve their performance in school? According to Dr. Jeff Howard, the founder of the Efficacy Institute, "People who support the Innate Ability Theory believe that a person's ability and character are fixed at birth; that is, it cannot be changed. Either 'you have it or you don't,' or 'some groups have it, and others don't.' The individual has no control because there is nothing that he or she can do to improve his/her intellectual ability and character because these are based on something innate and fixed. Failure or difficulty indicates limits in the individual's ability."

Another outside negative force is negative presuppositions about Hispanic students. There are many students, especially Hispanics and African-Americans, whose ability to believe in themselves has been damaged by people's negative presuppositions about their races or ethnicities.

People's perceptions can be negative because Hispanic and African American people are overly represented in the low socio-economic neighborhoods, dead-end low-paying jobs, the penal system, and lower academic tracks. When students are confronted by these realities, it affects their ability to believe that they can achieve more than what others of their same-race or ethnicity have achieved. Negative presuppositions are belief killers!

During a focus group conversation that I had with a group of Hispanic high school students, one student said: "When you are joking around with students, you hear sometimes jokes that say 'Come down and mow my lawn.' There are racist jokes like that. Mexicans mowing lawns, being janitors and stuff like that. It makes you think, what are you doing here? Why are you trying to complete school if that is what you might end up doing? That is where racism plays a role. It deteriorates your motivation, and it does not help you want to try as hard as you should."

Parents need the tools to overcome these outside negative forces and belief killers.

PARENTS EXPECT THEIR CHILDREN TO DO WELL IN SCHOOL

Parents must not only believe in their children's ability to learn, but also expect them to do well in school. This means setting high academic expectations for their children. If you ask 100 Hispanic parents, eighty percent of them wish their kids would go to college. But, only forty percent of them really expect them to do so. There is a big difference between a desire and an expectation.

This gap between desire and expectation has been articulated again and again by Hispanic high school students during the numerous focus groups that I have conducted over the past five years nationwide. According to the hundreds of students I have interviewed, one of the reasons behind the lack of achievement among Hispanic students is their parents' low academic expectations. Their parents did not have high expectations about their children's academic performance because, "… deep inside, they do not believe in their kids' potential to learn," one student said.

In reference to this, another student said, "It has a lot to do with the parents. White students' parents are involved in their students' education. They care a lot about their grades. In my case, my parents are satisfied if I get a C, as long as I pass the class. Hispanic parents care, but not that much. They do not expect their kids to try as hard as they should. Most Hispanic parents have lower expectations. White parents make their children work harder; they want the best. They are not satisfied with a C."

Students believe, and I agree with them, that there are several reasons for some parents' low academic expectations. The two primary reasons were their parents' personal lack of academic achievement and their lack of understanding of the American Educational System.

"Because they personally did not do well in school, they think their children will also struggle," one student said.

And another student added, "My parents don't expect more because they don't understand how the system works here in the United States. If their children progress from one grade to the other, or simply pass a class they believe their kids are doing well."

It simply does not register with many Hispanic parents that their kids could be passing courses or being promoted to another grade without learning what they needed to learn. This lack of understanding of the educational system does not allow many Hispanic parents to set higher expectations for their children.

PARENTS UNDERSTAND HOW THEIR CHILDREN LEARN

Not only teachers, but also parents, must know how children learn- how children can reach proficiency in any academic subject. Dr. Howard promotes through the Efficacy Institute, that "Smart is not something you are, but something that you can become through effective effort."

I completely agree with that! It is up to us. Students can reach or increase their proficiency in any academic subject if they commit, focus, work hard, pay attention to feedback, and strategize accordingly. Students must:

- Commit to reaching their academic goals. When students are committed, their actions will demonstrate their determination to stay the course.

- Stay focused and avoid distractions. Students who focus avoid diversions when engaged in activities that will allow them to reach their academic goals.

- Work hard in learning what they need to learn. Learning is a process that requires effort. Nothing worth it in life, including knowledge, comes easy.

- Pay consideration to their teachers' feedback. Students must use their performance on previous assignments and tests as a source of information to improve. They can't improve if they don't know where to improve.

- Learn to strategize. Students who strategize use their teachers' feedback to answer the question, "What can I do differently to have better outcomes?" Then, they can stay the course.

Let's apply it. If Jose's goal is to earn an A in his chemistry class, he will demonstrate his commitment by pulling out all the stops and doing whatever is necessary to reach that goal. He is determined. He is serious! When he is attending class, doing his chemistry homework, or studying for a test, he will resist the temptation to engage in activities that could divert his attention, such as using the phone, texting, or watching television. Jose knows that learning chemistry is not easy, so he will work hard in order to learn the content of the course. He will pay attention to his homework and test results to see where he did well and where he needs to improve and learn from it. Finally, he will use the lessons learned through feedback to think and decide on new ways, or strategies, to improve his performance in the chemistry class, to stay the course and reach his goal of an A.

STRATEGIES FOR PARENTS TO HELP THEIR CHILDREN LEARN.

We want all children to achieve academic success. For this to happen, parents must support at home what we do in school. As I have discussed in this chapter, parents can better support their children's education when they believe in their children's ability to learn; expect their children to achieve academic success; and, develop a good understanding of how children can reach proficiency in any academic subject. The following three strategies can help parents do just that:

1. Not judge their children through the lens of their personal experiences;
2. Develop in their children a positive attitude toward schoolwork; and,
3. Create the right home environment.

STRATEGY # 1: NOT JUDGE THEIR CHILDREN THROUGH THE LENS OF THEIR PERSONAL EXPERIENCES

First, parents should be taught not to judge their children's academic challenges through the lens of their personal experiences in school. Parents must never tell their children they do not have the ability to excel in school because they "don't have the genes," or indicate to their children that they were not born smart enough to do well in school. If parents struggled in school when they were children and think that they themselves are not smart enough, they may pass that belief on to their children, who pass it on to their children from one generation to the next.

STRATEGY # 2: DEVELOP A POSITIVE ATTITUDE TOWARD SCHOOLWORK

Parents must be given tools to help their children develop the kind of attitude needed to achieve academic success. Doing well in school may require some sacrifices. Good grades or high test scores do not always come easily. Parents must learn how to help their children maintain the right attitude, especially when confronted with academic challenges. Complaining about school or criticizing the teacher will not help their students learn.

Calling their children derogatory names does not help either. Some Hispanic parents have a bad habit of calling their children "burros" [donkeys] when their children have a hard time doing their homework, do poorly on tests, or fail a class. This is simply unproductive and unacceptable! During my workshops, I always tell Hispanic parents that every time they call their children "burros," they are calling themselves "burros" because only "burros" can have "burritos" (little donkeys). Parent should teach their children the character traits that will allow them to succeed academically. Students must learn to be responsible and persistent, work hard, and delay immediate gratification for longer-term goals. Students who have developed these character traits will exhibit the kind of attitude that is needed to do well in school. I explain these character traits more in detail in Chapter Ten.

STRATEGY # 3: CREATE THE RIGHT HOME ENVIRONMENT

Parents must learn how to create an environment at home that supports learning by knowing what to do at home to support their children's academic development. I have learned that parents of students identified as gifted do exactly what I just stated here. And then I ask myself, why are these students gifted? Is it that they have superior ability to learn compared to their peers? Or, is it that they are raised in a "gifted" environment? I will let you answer that question.

In the same way that a young plant needs soil, water and light to grow, parents need to believe in their kids' potential, expect them to succeed in school, and understand how their children can reach proficiency in any academic endeavor. Parents must never judge their children's academic performance based on their own personal experiences. It is imperative that they help their children develop the kind of attitude that is needed to achieve academic success. Finally, they must create a home environment in which their children can develop academically. Parents, who are competent in helping their children achieve a quality education, do exactly that. Their children can grow to be what they were designed to be by our Creator.

CHAPTER 7

COMPETENCY # 7: CONNECT WITH TEACHERS

Parents are able to establish positive and productive connections with their children's teachers.

"Something that the school could do to help out more Latinos is to get their parents involved in school. The teachers cannot do it alone. They can be given some education on how school works so they can help us because ultimately they are our parents and in many cases our biggest influence in life." – Yolanda, Hispanic High School Student

COMPETENCY # 7: CONNECT WITH TEACHERS

It is very challenging for teachers to help their students achieve proficiency, in any academic subject, without the right kind of support from their students' parents. They need to work in collaboration with their students' parents. That is why it is so important that this parent-teacher relationship exists in a way that is both positive and productive.

Hispanic immigrant parents are much more likely to face challenges when connecting with their kids' teachers. During all my parent workshops I always say, "When it comes to your children's education, you are in the driver's seat." Parents are responsible for getting their kids a quality education; parent-teacher connections can prevent parents from getting lost in the process of doing so. There is a series of strategies that I suggest to facilitate the establishment of positive and productive parent-teacher connections.

THE CHALLENGE OF CONNECTING WITH THE TEACHERS

As a Hispanic mom who immigrated to the United States in 1990, I have to admit that being able to connect with the teachers of my three children was an overwhelming experience. Since I was born and raised in Latin America, I did not understand the American mainstream culture. I knew a lot about other educational systems in Latin America, but very little about the American educational system. I was not proficient enough in the English language to effectively communicate with my children's teachers. Most of all, I did not have the right frame of reference. My perceptions of the teachers and of myself deterred me from connecting with my children's teachers in an effective manner. For me, it was a huge challenge.

DISCONNECTED IS BEING LOST

Imagine parents moving to a new city. They need to get their children to school. They are in the driver's seat. They are responsible for getting them to the right place and on time. What happens if they don't know their way around the new city? What if they get lost? Parents who are not properly connected with their children's teachers are likely to get lost in the process of ensuring a quality education for their children.

None of us like the feeling of being lost when we are in the driver's seat, especially when we are not alone and our passengers depend on us to get where they need to be, right? If parents are responsible for managing their children's education, what can they do when they find themselves lost in the process of doing so? The solution is to stop and ask for directions. I always teach parents during Hispanic parent workshops that the first and most qualified person to approach for directions in managing a child's education is the child's teacher. I always tell parents that teachers are like GPSs (Global Positioning

Systems). Teachers know exactly where their students are. Teachers can provide parents with step-by-step directions on how to get their children where they need to be.

A WIN-WIN-WIN SITUATION

I strongly believe in parent-teacher connections. Tshey encourage win-win-win situations. The parent wins, the teacher wins, and most of all the student wins. The problem or challenge loses. Parents win because they gain their confidence and learn information to develop a strategy to fulfill their role. Children win because they get on the track that leads to academic success and a quality education. The teachers win because they learn about parents' effort at home to support their kids' education so teachers know how to support what parents are doing at home. The problem loses. Sometimes it loses big time – to the degree that it is no longer a problem.

STRATEGIES TO CONNECT WITH THE TEACHERS

The question that we must ask ourselves is: What do parents need to do to establish positive and productive connections with their children's teachers? In the seminars that I hold for Hispanic parents, I teach them the following four strategies:

1. Connect with their children's teachers as early as possible.
2. Make sure that the teachers are properly informed about what is going on in their children's lives.

3. Maintain an overly positive attitude toward school, the teachers, and schoolwork.

4. Know how to carry out a parent-teacher conference.

STRATEGY # 1: CONNECT WITH THEIR CHILDREN'S TEACHERS AS EARLY AS POSSIBLE.

Parents must connect with their children's teachers as early as possible. I tell parents to connect during the first week of school if possible. Parents should not wait until the school's annual Open House event. An event like this provides neither parents, nor the teachers, with an opportunity to have meaningful conversations. If parents cannot stop by the school during that first month of school to introduce themselves, they should, at least, send a note to the teacher. If parents are not proficient enough in English to write a comprehensible note, they must find a person to help them write that introductory letter. The note can be as short and simple as the following:

Dear Teacher,

I am the mother of Jose Rodriguez, one of your Algebra 1 students. Please, feel free to contact me anytime you feel there is a need. I can be reached anytime on my cell at 000-000-000. I really support whatever you do to help my child be successful in school.

Sincerely yours,

Mrs. Rodriguez

The Efficacy Institute reports that in a study conducted with families from a Chicago housing project, the parents who introduced themselves to teachers and stayed in touch with the school during the year had the most successful students. It did not matter whether the family consisted of a single parent or two. Studies have shown that teachers are likely to pay more attention to students when they know that the parents show interest in their children's education. As a veteran teacher, I know that teachers can help students better when they know that they are welcomed to engage the parents.

STRATEGY # 2: ENSURE THAT THE TEACHERS ARE INFORMED ABOUT THEIR CHILDREN'S LIVES

The second strategy that parents can implement is to make sure that the teacher is properly informed about what is going on in their children's lives. I teach parents that they must inform teachers about family events that could have an impact in their children's lives. If something is going on in the family, like death, divorce, a job lost, etc., which may have a negative impact on their children's schoolwork and/or behavior, the parents must let the teachers know. The teachers can help students cope with these adverse circumstances that could affect their performance in school. Conversely, if positive events are occurring in the family like the birth of a sibling, a birthday or a "quinceañera" [15th Birthday] celebration, team championship, etc., that may have a positive impact on a child's emotional welfare, they must let the teachers know. The teachers can magnify the positive impact of these constructive events by publicly acknowledging them in their classrooms.

STRATEGY # 3: MAINTAIN AN OVERTLY POSITIVE ATTITUDE

I teach parents that they must maintain an overtly positive attitude toward school, the teachers, and school work. This is more likely to happen if parents have already connected with their children's teachers, school administrators and other staff members since they know them a little better. A parent can be explicit when they praise their children's teachers, school administrators, school events and even the building facilities in front of their children. We know as educators that attitudes are contagious, right? If children see that their parents are pleased with the school and their teachers, they are more likely to adopt the same positive attitude.

On the other hand, it is even more powerful when, for example, parents let the teachers and school administrators know how much their children enjoyed a school project, how excited their children were about something they learned in school, how much fun their children had in a field trip, etc. The reality is that too many parents only contact teachers when there is a problem or to complain about something. This creates tension in the parent-teacher connection. That tension is counterproductive.

STRATEGY # 4: KNOW HOW TO CARRY OUT A PARENT-TEACHER CONFERENCE

Parents must be able to effectively participate in a parent-teacher conference. Remember the metaphor of getting lost when driving the child to school? When a parent meets with the teacher in a parent-teacher conference, in a sense, the teacher takes out a map.

The teacher might say, "This is where your child is academically." Then, the teacher points to another location and says, "This is where your child needs to be" and then explains how the student will get there.

Parents must understand that they are less likely to become lost in the process of monitoring their children's education when they participate in parent-teacher conferences and find out how their children are doing and what they can do to help their children improve their performance in school. What can parents do to ensure that the parent-teacher conference is productive? I would like to provide the following ten proven-to-work recommendations to ensure success:

1. When a teacher requests a conference, parents must make it a priority. They have to make time to go, even if they are busy. No excuses!

2. Before the parent-teacher conference, parents must ask questions to clarify the problem or the reason for the conference. Parents must review their child's work and grades to know what questions to ask, and then write those questions down to ensure that they will be addressed.

3. Parents must go to the conference prepared to ask specific questions such as:

- What kind of subject does my child like the best?
- Is my child working at grade level?
- What is my child's reading level?
- Does my child participate in class?
- What can I do to help my child improve?

4. If the teacher says something that parents do not understand during the parent-teacher conference, they must ask the teacher to explain it. Parents must be aware that teachers are willing and very good at explaining things.

5. Parents must know that teachers are held accountable for all their students' academic performance. The teacher's goal is the academic success of all students; therefore, parents must affirm that they and the teacher have the same goal for the student.

6. Parents must stay focused on the purpose of the meeting and keep moving forward.

7. When parents describe a problem to the teacher, they must do it in a way that does not blame the teacher. Parents must ask questions rather than make accusations and never become defensive or try to justify themselves or their children.

8. Parents must really pay attention to what the teacher is saying and, while listening, must think about what the

teacher is saying, rather than thinking about what they want to say next.

9. Before the conference is over, parents and teachers must develop the next steps to solve the problem and a plan to ensure success.

10. Parents must never forget to have patience in solving problems and to celebrate improvements when they happen.

It is imperative that Hispanic parents understand that the American educational system works best for students when parents are involved in their children's education. Positive and productive parent-teacher connections are the backbone of the kind of parental involvement schools need. When parents and schools collaborate, all parties win - students, teachers, and parents. The strategies I shared can help parents know how to make the connection happen.

Parents must sit in the driver's seat when it comes to their children's education. They are in charge and responsible for helping their children reach their academic destinations. To avoid getting lost in the process, sometimes parents need to stop and ask for directions. Teachers, like a GPS, know where students are and the route to take to get them where they need to be.

CHAPTER 8

COMPETENCY # 8: MAKE READING A LIFESTYLE

Parents make reading part of their family's lifestyle.

"It is very hard for me to do my homework because I have a hard time understanding what the book says. The teacher wants us to read the whole chapter and then answer the questions at the end of the chapter. It takes me a long time because I read too slow and have to read the same thing again and again until I get it. I never liked to read. I read like a middle school kid, below grade level. At least that's what my reading teacher says. I take a reading class now." - Antonio, Hispanic High School Student

COMPETENCY # 8: MAKE READING A LIFESTYLE

If the door to a quality life is a quality education, then the door to a quality education is reading proficiency. Reading is at the heart of education because reading proficiency is one of the leading indicators of academic success. This is why I teach parents to make reading a lifestyle.

Parents must learn that making reading a lifestyle is beyond taking a reading course, reading to complete a homework assignment, or reading to prepare for a test. Reading as a lifestyle means consistently spending time reading to become better informed, to develop as an individual, or simply for pleasure. When reading becomes a part of a person's daily routine, then we can say that it is a lifestyle. When reading becomes a lifestyle, it opens the doors to the thoughts of the wise. It opens the doors to the counsel of people who have the information which students and their parents need to bridge the gap between where they are and where they should be. It is for these reasons that I believe that parents' ability for making reading a family lifestyle should be one of the competencies they must demonstrate.

READING IS LEVERAGE

My "consuegro" [daughter's father-in-law], Rick Hubbard, who is a passionate reader, says that reading is like a car jack. If you're driving down the road and hear a thumping sound and feel car vibrations, it's probably because you have a flat tire. Hopefully, you have in your trunk what you need to fix the problem, a car jack. A car jack is very small, when compared to the car, but it has powerful leverage, right? You place the car jack in the right place and begin to turn the handle. Little efforts leveraged repeatedly can lift thousands of pounds. The tire gets changed, and you are back on the road. According to my consuegro, that is what  reading does when it becomes a lifestyle. It lifts a lot of academic weight. If reading is so powerful, what is deterring so many Hispanic parents from making reading a lifestyle for themselves and their children? There are some barriers that deter parents from making reading a lifestyle.

BARRIERS HISPANIC PARENTS MUST OVERCOME

One barrier is that sometimes reading is not valued at home. A significant number of Hispanic children are raised in home environments where reading is simply not practiced or part of their families' daily activities. As harsh as this may sound, it is the reality in many Hispanic homes. To illustrate this point, I will use myself as an example. As a child, my mother never read books to me. My mom used to tell me many stories, especially at bedtime, but she never actually read to me. I learned how to read for the first time when I reached the elementary grades and used my limited reading skills just to complete assignments or to prepare for tests. By the time I graduated high school, I was reading several years below grade level. My freshman year of college courses consisted mostly of preparatory classes.

When reading is valued at home, it starts at a very early age. For example, when I fly out-of-state, I see many young children traveling with their parents pulling their Spider Man or Dora carry-on bags. They carry their favorite toy, some snacks and books, lots of them. While waiting for boarding at the gate, they are either reading or being read to by their parents. I hear the parents ask them questions such as: "What was the book about? What did you like about that book?" Or "What did you learn from the book?" These are the children who are learning to value reading at an early age, and reading is becoming a lifestyle for them.

With their parents, these children practice decoding, learn new vocabulary, build up fluency, and most of all develop reading comprehension skills. Their kids can likely read well by the time they are in first grade and maintain at or above grade level reading proficiency throughout their academic careers. Through intentional persuasive communication, we must help Hispanic parents see the value of reading and make it a lifestyle.

Another barrier is that parents might have a different idea of what reading proficiency means. As a veteran teacher, I have realized that the meaning attributed to reading proficiency, or what a competent reader is, has changed through the years. When I was child, being able to read mostly meant "decoding"; that is reading words and sentences.

During that time, competency was demonstrated by reading lines and answering very basic questions. After reading a children's story such as "The Three Little Pigs," students would answer questions such as: "How many little pigs were in the story?" or, "What materials did the pigs use to build their houses?" Many parents are not aware that the meaning of a competent reader has changed.

Today in the United States and throughout the world, a proficient reader is considered a person who not only can read lines, but can also read between and above lines. What do I mean by that? Students must go beyond just decoding. Students must now be able to comprehend what they are reading. Reading comprehension requires students to 1) find the meaning of an "unknown" word within the context; 2) find information, data or facts within the text to defend an idea or explain a concept; and, 3) infer or predict from what they read in the text. All of these reading comprehension skills require a great repertoire of vocabulary, reading fluency, and endurance.

Returning to "The Three Little Pigs" story, students have the ability to answer questions such as: "What do you think the pigs could have done to prevent being eaten by the wolf?" or "What do you think the author of the story was trying to teach us?" Through parent training, we must help our Hispanic parents understand what reading proficiency means today.

An additional barrier is that most Hispanic parents are not aware that the schools are being held accountable for the students' lack of reading proficiency. They do not understand that the schools are being held accountable for their children's performance in the state accountability tests, which assess reading and mathematics. Since reading proficiency is a must-have skill to do well in many other academic subjects, a great portion of the states' accountability tests assess the reading comprehension skills.

Since the NCLB Act, schools across the nation are implementing programs to help students read at grade level or reach proficiency as measured by their states' assessments. But, most immigrant parents are not even aware of the existence of this law. They do not understand the seriousness of the state's accountability test and the impact that low reading test scores can have on the school's state and federal academic status. Teachers and school administrators often face the challenge of helping all students reach proficiency in reading with little or no support from their parents, which I consider unacceptable.

Not too long ago, I facilitated a community forum in one of the Chicago suburbs to inform the community regarding the NCLB Act and the state's accountability test. Two-hundred plus Hispanic parents attended the meeting. During the meeting, I was politely interrupted by a parent who said, "Dr. Lourdes, I am very concerned. Why is it that I never heard about this law before, this NCLB law? I don't understand. Why is the school being blamed for my child's score on that test you are talking about? You know, we don't have that in Mexico. Where I come from if my child does not pass, it is his fault, or my fault, but never the teacher's fault. The teachers in my child's school are good teachers, and I know they do everything they can. If we parents knew that the school would be in trouble because of that test, we would have done something about it. Maybe, get our kids to read more or something. I don't know. I just think that if this is so serious, parents should do more at home to help the teachers and the school."

I believe in shared responsibility. School administrators must inform parents about the states' accountability tests. Parents must be involved in the process of helping students reach reading proficiency, as measured by their states. They must also be held accountable for the support role they must play in their children's education.

A final barrier is that parents are not aware of the long-term negative effects of children reading below grade level. Medical doctors consider "high blood pressure" a silent killer. At a certain age, blood pressure needs to be monitored because, if it's too high, it can kill us. I believe that the lack of reading proficiency is also a silent killer. Students who are reading one or two years below grade level when they are in fourth grade and do not receive immediate and effective interventions, are likely to be three or four years behind by the time they enter middle school. Can you guess how many years behind these same students are going to be when they reach high school? Too many!

Parents must be informed that the lack of reading proficiency does not allow high school students to understand their textbooks, participate in class, do their homework or perform well on college admission tests. Poor readers will have a hard time passing the reading portion of the state accountability tests, and this will have an adverse impact on the schools they attend. Lack of reading proficiency is a source of great frustration. That is why, I believe, so many poor readers opt to drop out of school. At least for me, low reading skills are like high blood pressure; they are silent, but they can kill a child's opportunity for a better future.

We must inform parents with a sense of urgency if their children are reading below grade. They must understand the gravity of their children's academic health.

SHORT AND LONG TERM BENEFITS OF READING

Awareness of the huge short-term and long-term benefits of reading proficiency should motivate Hispanic parents to overcome the barriers. Dr. Stephen Krashen, an expert in linguistics says, "Those who do not develop a reading habit simply don't have a chance; they will have a very difficult time reading and writing at a level high enough to deal with the demands of today's world." Parents must know that a student, who is a strong reader, is more likely to do well in school because reading:

1. Exposes students to new vocabulary within a context, which makes it easier for them to remember and comprehend.

2. Helps students become better spellers because they see the word and how it is used.

3. Teaches students the structure of the language, which is how to put words together and create sentences.

4. Helps students learn how to organize their thoughts and how to communicate effectively with other people, even with people from other cultures.

5. Provides students with a strong base for improving their writing skills.

6. Helps students become better researchers through greater access to information in books, articles and the Internet.

7. Teaches students how to think independently of their peers.

8. Provides students with information that could help them participate in interesting conversations.

9. Promotes critical thinking, which is essential in today's society.

As you can see, reading in school helps. But reading as a lifestyle, when it is repeated over and over again, is where the heavy lifting power is. It is just like a car jack.

HOME STRATEGIES TO INCREASE READING PROFICIENCY

There are seven strategies I teach Hispanic parents to employ to help their children develop reading as a lifestyle:

1. Parents must set an example. They must read on a regular basis, not just newspapers or magazines, but also books. There is a lot of good reading material available for parents

to read to improve themselves. They could choose to read in English or in Spanish; it does not matter.

2. Parents must encourage and expect their children to read. Parents must understand that reading is more important today than it has ever been before. Reading is crucial for students to achieve academic success, succeed in their chosen careers, become informed citizen, and grow in all aspects of their lives.

3. Parents must have books and other reading materials in their homes, especially in their children's rooms. They don't have to spend a lot of money. With a library card, parents and their children can check out books for free if they return the books on time of course. There are also used bookstores where parents can buy great books for pennies on the dollar. Kids' books are often available at the Goodwill store or garage sales.

4. Parents can provide their children with books such as Tales of Narnia, My Sister's Keeper, Lord of the Rings, etc., which have been made into movies. Then, as a celebration for reading the books, take them to the movie theater, rent a video, or watch a movie on cable TV.

5. Parents must turn off all competing media. They must turn off the computer, video games, television, radio, and stereo system - even put their phones and their children's phones on silent. I think that the same way that junk food spoils

the appetite for healthy food, other competing media can spoil the appetite for reading.

6. Parents must read to their children before they can read to themselves. The key is to start when the children are very young. According to Dr. Ruth Love, American schools would be revolutionized if parents "would just read to their preschool children fifteen minutes a day."

7. Parents must learn how to approach their children's teacher to ask about the different standardized reading tests that their children take throughout the years, their children's reading scores and levels of proficiency on those tests, and strategies that they can implement at home to help their children become better readers.

Allow me to share the story of a mom who overcame enormous challenges and developed strategies to help her kids become proficient readers. Her name is Sonya Carson, the mother of one of the most prominent pediatric surgeons in the world, Dr. Ben Carson.

Ms. Carson raised Ben and his brother in the inner city of Detroit. She often worked two or three jobs as a domestic to provide for her two sons. She worked so hard that she would occasionally travel to a relative's home just to get some rest. In contrast to the hard work she invested in her job, her sons displayed anything but hard work, as could be seen in their poor school grades. Ben was her youngest and had the worst grades in his class. But Sonya knew she had to do something about it. She decided to apply to her son's education the same "can-do" attitude that she put into her work.

She told them, "Kids, you are better than these grades." She eliminated playtime and limited television time to three hours per week. Instead of watching TV, she took them to the library. She understood the value and the benefits of reaching reading proficiency. As a strategy, each of her kids had to select two books. Then, they were required to provide her with a book report for each book. What fascinates me about Sonya's story is that in spite of the huge challenges she was facing in life, she had high academic expectations for her children and demanded appropriate behavior from them. The lack of education and financial resources did not prevent this African American single mother from assuming responsibility for her children's education.

Sonya was in charge of her children. She was in the driver's seat and her efforts paid off. Their grades began to climb. Ben graduated from high school ranking third in his class. He went on to Yale, followed by the University of Michigan and John Hopkins University. Today, as Benjamin S. Carson Sr., a famous pediatric neurosurgeon, he is known for separating two Guatemalan girls joined at the head. Sonya Carson definitely discovered the power of making reading a lifestyle.

What is incredible about this woman is that she made her two sons read two books a week and write book reports for her when she never attended middle school and never graduated from high school. Sonya only had a third grade education and could only read part of what her kids wrote. If Sonya could train her sons to adopt reading as a lifestyle, every parent can do the same thing for their children.

If we want parents to support at home what we educators do in school, then we must make them aware and accountable for helping their kids be competent readers. Parents must understand the barriers they must overcome, the short-term and long-term benefits of reading, and the home strategies to increase reading proficiency to help their children become habitual readers by making reading a lifestyle. Reading will help them lift academic weight like that car jack does a car.

I strongly believe that, in the end, what may separate children from a quality life is not their race or ethnicity, their country of birth, how much money their family makes, or where they live because a person who has adopted reading as a lifestyle can rise above all obstacles and experience a quality education and reach a quality life. Let's teach Hispanic parents how to accomplish this.

CHAPTER # 9

COMPETENCY # 9: MAKE HOMEWORK A ROUTINE

Parents make homework completion part of their child's daily routine.

"My dad tells us that if we want to study and do our homework, to do it and if we don't, then to not do it. But my mom is more supportive; she is the one making sure we go to school, do our work and have everything we need. Kids that don't do their homework mess up their GPA. And then what can they do? Where would they go?" - Yolanda, Hispanic High School Student

COMPETENCY # 9: MAKE HOMEWORK A ROUTINE

I believe that parents must make homework completion part of their children's daily routine and not a daily battle. As an educator, you probably recognize that getting students to turn in their homework has become a classroom combat zone. Teachers cannot do it alone. At the same time, we recognize that homework supervision is one of the most challenging areas in the parental role. Parents must become aware that practice is to a soccer championship what homework is to academic achievement. This is why I believe that parents' ability to make  homework completion part of their children's daily routine is one of the competencies parents must demonstrate.

Parents are in the driver's seat when it comes to their children's education and are ultimately responsible for getting their children to the right academic destinations. When children refuse to do their homework, they are trying to grab the steering wheel and go where they want to go - not where they need to go. This is unacceptable.

REASONS WHY HOMEWORK COMPLETION CAN BE A DAILY BATTLE

During my Hispanic parental involvement seminars for teachers and administrators, I go through the five most salient reasons why supervising homework completion is so challenging for many

Hispanic parents to the point where it becomes a daily battle. These reasons are:

1. Parents over-sympathize with their children.
2. Parents have very strong-willed children.
3. Students do not enjoy doing homework.
4. Students lack the English language skills.
5. Parents lack the English language skills or educational background.

REASON # 1: PARENTS OVER-SYMPATHIZE WITH THEIR CHILDREN.

One of the reasons why so many parents, in general, have such a hard time ensuring homework completion is because they over-sympathize with their children. As a veteran teacher, I know that children of any race or ethnicity and at any age or grade level, might tell their parents, "The teacher did not leave us any homework today," "This homework is too hard," "I do not know how to do this homework," or "The teacher didn't explain to me how to do it." I have learned that some parents buy into their children's reasons for not doing homework because they struggled with homework themselves when they were children. They see themselves in their children. I often hear arguments such as: "Dr. Lourdes, you do not understand. I really feel sorry for my child. I was just like him when I was a child. I did not like school. I used to hate homework. Like father like son."

REASON # 2: PARENTS HAVE VERY STRONG-WILLED CHILDREN.

Sometimes it is hard for parents to get their children to complete their homework because they have very strong-willed children and simply give up on the homework battle. Let's consider Jose, a fourth grade Hispanic student who always gets away with not doing his homework. This is a typical scenario. Carmen, Jose's mother, is a hard-working mother who gets involved in a homework battle with Jose every night. This usually lasts 30 minutes. Jose knows, that after thirty minutes, his mom will be too tired to battle anymore; it is one more night that Jose gets away with it and simply does what he chooses. I have seen too many students like Jose. They want to have fun rather than do homework. And, when this happens, who has control of the steering wheel?

REASON # 3: STUDENTS DO NOT ENJOY DOING HOMEWORK.

Another reason why homework can become a daily battle, instead of a daily routine, is because children usually do not enjoy doing homework - as simple as that. They will wait until it is bedtime to do it versus earlier when they were talking on the phone, texting, playing video games, listening to music, watching TV, using Facebook or "Skyping" with friends. While children are not making good decisions, their parents are overly stressed or too busy to focus on their children's homework or any test preparation. It is especially difficult if families have more than one child.

REASON # 4: STUDENTS LACK THE ENGLISH LANGUAGE SKILLS.

Homework time can also be very difficult for English Language Learner (ELL) students. It can take an ELL student two hours or more to complete a one-hour assignment. I know by experience that ELL students miss a lot of content in class when their academic English is not at grade-level. These students are learning content and language at the same time. Doing homework can be a very challenging experience for ELL students and, without assistance, it can also be a source of stress and frustration.

REASON # 5: PARENTS LACK THE ENGLISH LANGUAGE SKILLS OR EDUCATIONAL BACKGROUND.

Some Hispanic students also struggle doing homework because their parents lack the language skills and/or the educational background needed to provide any kind of guidance or academic assistance to their children. Students feel like they are on their own when it comes to homework. In one of the student focus groups that I conducted not long ago, a high school student said to me, "When it comes to homework, Dr. Lourdes, I am on my own. My parents don't know English; I mean 'nada' [nothing]. So I don't get any help like many of the kids here do, especially White students. Their parents speak English and also went to school themselves. My parents never graduated. They just finished elementary school."

STRATEGIES TO MAKE HOMEWORK TIME PART OF A CHILD'S ROUTINE

The question that we now need to ask ourselves is: If parents are in the driver's seat when it comes to their children's education, how can we help them take back control of the steering wheel? As educators we must help parents learn the strategies they need to make homework time a positive and productive experience and part of their children's daily routine. Parents must:

1. See the value of homework.
2. Persuade their children to see the value of homework.
3. Create a home environment that is conducive to homework completion.
4. Establish a regular homework schedule.
5. Never do their children's homework.
6. Make homework time a positive experience.
7. Establish homework guidelines.
8. Teach their children how to organize homework.
9. Motivate their children to seek help from their teachers.
10. Connect with their children's teachers.

STRATEGY # 1: SEE THE VALUE OF HOMEWORK.

Parents must be aware that homework needs to be valued at home. Period! We can never assume that all parents understand how beneficial it is for children to complete their homework assignments. The way that they perceive this academic practice is based on their personal frame of reference or life experiences, especially those related to their own school years when they were young. Parents who have a strong academic background are more likely to see the value of homework than those who have not succeeded in this area. All parents must know that children who do their homework achieve greater academic success than those who do not.

When schools have me speak during Hispanic family nights, I share with parents (especially the fathers) that homework completion is to academic success as drills and practice are to sports. In any sport, the ultimate goal of an athlete or a sport team is the championship. But to make it to the championship, an athlete or a team needs to participate in numerous and intensive practices and win many regular games leading up to that desired championship. In education, that championship is a post-secondary education. Students must practice their academics through homework and achieve many academic successes leading to graduation. Most parents understand the value of practice in sports. On the other hand, few parents understand the value of homework. We need to convince them to value homework. Parents must understand that homework completion is what supports getting a quality education.

Homework helps students pick up information that they could have missed in class, correct their mistakes and fill in gaps, reinforce what they have learned during class, be better prepared to take any test, and catch up if they have missed a class. Homework also allows teachers to know what the students don't understand and lets parents see incrementally how their children are progressing in school. Students who make homework completion part of their daily routines develop a habit that leads to lifelong learning.

STRATEGY # 2: PERSUADE THEIR CHILDREN TO SEE THE VALUE HOMEWORK

Once parents understand the value of homework and the role that this academic practice plays in their children's academic lives, they must, in a persuasive manner, instill and affirm the importance of making homework completion a priority in their children's academic lives. Parents can do this using the list of homework benefits, and with clarity and conviction explain each of those benefits to their children. This must be done as early as possible. The younger the child, the easier it will be to make homework time a habit and part of a child's daily routine. Someone once said that the best time to dig a well is before thirst comes. This process would also help students appreciate homework completion when their parents recognize and affirm their children when they see them focus in their schoolwork. It is even more important when they praise them for the commitment that they show when they are doing their school work. We all need recognition and maybe some praise, especially when we are doing the right thing.

STRATEGY # 3: CREATE A HOME ENVIRONMENT THAT IS CONDUCIVE TO HOMEWORK COMPLETION.

Parents must also create an environment at home in which students can focus on their homework assignments. During homework time, parents must put all phones on silent and turn off the TV. It is very hard for students to focus when they are surrounded by so many distractions. Being able to focus is the key to a productive homework time. Parents must create or find a place at home where their children can do homework without being disturbed. There is no need to have a big house or a room dedicated just for homework. The study place can be the dining table, as long as the table provides children with enough space to put their school materials. The good thing about using the dining room, as opposed to a private room, is that parents can keep an eye on their children and be available for assistance in case they need it. By the way, it is a good idea if parents have all of the materials that students might need, such as pencils, sharpeners, and paper, in a convenient place to avoid interruptions and use homework time in a more efficient manner.

STRATEGY # 4: ESTABLISH A REGULAR HOMEWORK SCHEDULE

Parents can also make homework a positive and productive time if they set up a regular schedule that the entire family can work around. I really mean the entire family. I advise parents to set the time for the late afternoon or early evening, rather than just before bed. Not long, ago I conducted a series focus group interviews at one of the elementary school districts in West Chicago. One of the students who participated said to me, "I don't want to do my homework in my bedroom because I hate to be alone. I prefer the dining table because my mom is right there cooking. But there is so much noise. The TV is so loud and my mom talks on the phone all the time while she is cooking. She is kind of loud, you know. I wish I could concentrate, but there is too much noise. So, I give up, and then I get in trouble."

Even if children have little or no homework, parents must ask their children to use that time set aside for homework to read or write. The idea is to make homework time part of their children's daily routine. Homework time needs to become a daily habit. This strategy can also teach children not to rush through homework just to get it over with.

STRATEGY # 5: NEVER DO THEIR CHILDREN'S HOMEWORK.

Parents must make themselves available in case their children need them, but only offer help if they need it. Parents have to be careful, because if they help too much or do the homework for them, their kids will never develop the self-assurance that they can do it themselves. I must confess, in my almost twenty years of experience as a mathematics instructor, I have seen too many parents providing their children so much homework assistance that students did not benefit from this academic practice. Students become dependent on their parents and do not develop the academic behavior that will ensure future academic success.

The problem with parents providing too much assistance during homework is that teachers might start noticing a discrepancy between the students' performance in homework assignments and their performance in testing situations. They end up getting excellent grades in their homework assignments and poor grades in their classroom assessments. I find this discrepancy unacceptable. The goal is for their children to learn, and for that, they need to be able to work independently.

I was hired, not long ago, to conduct a series of student focus groups and interviews to find out, from the students' perspectives, the reasons behind students earning D's and F's in their core academic subjects. Students consistently expressed that many of those earning better grades did so because their parents were doing the homework for them or with them. In their core subjects, a great percentage of the grade is based on work done out of the classroom, at home. With their parents' assistance, these students will earn at least a C, no matter how poorly they did on the classroom tests. A particular student said, "I hate it when I see them (students) getting A's and B's when I know they were on Facebook for hours the night before. But their parents help them so much that they finish all their homework in a short period of time. That is not my case, Dr. Lourdes. I don't get any help! I make mistakes and that lowers my grade. And even if I do well on the tests, my grade will not go up too much because tests are only like 30% of the grade. So, who is getting that A or B, the kids or their parents?"

STRATEGY # 6: MAKE HOMEWORK TIME A POSITIVE EXPERIENCE.

Parents must teach their children that the time they must spend doing homework should be a positive, "whining-free" zone. Students need to learn to ask for help without being negative about the homework, the teacher, or school in general. Expressions such as "I can't", "I won't" or "I don't" should be eliminated! A negative attitude about homework creates a lot of stress, for both the parent and the child. Stress has a negative impact on students' willingness and ability to learn and parents' willingness and ability to lead. It is very difficult for a parent to be in the driver's seat if he is stressed out.

STRATEGY # 7: ESTABLISH HOMEWORK GUIDELINES.

For homework time to become part of a child's daily routine and not a daily battle, parents must establish homework guidelines.

They must set up consequences ahead of time for not doing homework and discuss what privileges children will lose if homework is not completed. Most of all, children must know that they will be held accountable for not abiding to the pre-established guidelines set by their parents. If necessary, parents could develop a reward system. But this reward system must be balanced by reminding children that they are not doing their homework for the parents or for the teacher. The child, and not the parent, is the one who is going to reap the benefits of doing homework.

In a focus group interview that I conducted with a group of sixth graders, I asked students, "What can your parents do to help you improve your reading score on the state's accountability test?" I was surprised to hear that students wished their parents would provide more structure at home and consequences for not doing their homework. In particular one student said, "I wish my parents would not let me play video games or watch so much television. I wish they would reward me with something, you know, anything, like time to play if I do my homework and no time to play with my friends if I don't do it."

STRATEGY # 8: TEACH THEIR CHILDREN HOW TO ORGANIZE HOMEWORK

The next step parents can take is to teach their children how to organize their homework in a more productive way. For many students, homework can be an overwhelming experience. Students are likely to take mathematics, science, English, history, and some elective courses and receive homework from all these classes at the same time. Which assignment do they do first? Which one is easier? Which one is harder? Should I do the harder one first to get it out of the way? Will I be able to meet all my teachers' deadlines? All of these questions might be "screaming" inside of a student's head. I strongly believe that homework time should not only be a "whining-free zone," but also a "stress-free zone." It is for these reasons that parents must teach their children how to break the homework load into smaller pieces and deal with it a piece at a time.

Students must also be able to specifically describe what is it that they are supposed to do. If students experience difficulties, they must learn to describe what is it that they do not understand, rather than whining and coming up with generalizations such as – "It is too hard" or "I cannot do this." Students must learn to experiment with different ways of solving homework problems.

STRATEGY # 9: MOTIVATE THEIR CHILDREN TO SEEK HELP FROM THEIR TEACHERS.

Hispanic parents must motivate their children to approach their teachers for extra help if they find themselves struggling with their homework. But the problem that we have here is that many Hispanic parents are not aware that teachers, in general, enjoy students who ask questions and show interest in what they are teaching. Most teachers are willing to go an extra mile to help a student who is seeking for help.

I must confess that when I was a high school math teacher, I tended to pay a little extra attention to students who came to me before class or who stopped me in the halls to say, "Ms. Ferrer, I had a real hard time with my math homework last night."

I know that, like me, many teachers like having students ask them questions about homework because it makes teachers feel like students really care about their class. When I saw that same student in class, guess what? I was extra careful in making sure that he understood the content presented in class and was ready, this time, to complete the next day's homework assignment.

Teachers and other students can also benefit from students asking questions. Teachers can gain insight about the difficulties their students are facing, improve their teaching, and implement new strategies to address these challenges. When students ask questions about homework, classmates also benefit from this. The challenges that students are facing during homework might have been the same challenges that a classmate is facing. The bottom line here is that students must learn to seek help from their teachers.

STRATEGY # 10: CONNECT WITH THEIR CHILDREN'S TEACHERS

Hispanic parents must develop trust and self-confidence to schedule a time to meet with the teacher if they think there are underlying issues that the teachers might not be aware of and that

could be affecting their child's ability to do homework. As I have said several times before, parents are in the driver's seat. They are responsible. If they get lost or need help in the process, connecting with a teacher to get help may be the best solution.

Supervising homework time is one of the most challenging activities in which a parent can engage. It is imperative that they do not turn the daily homework routine into a battle. When parents see the connection between homework and a quality education, they understand that this is a practical discipline that their children need for academic success. When I teach parents the right strategies, I see the understanding taking place and know that more Hispanic kids will complete their homework assignments. We must help parents internalize that practice is to a soccer championship what homework completion is to academic achievement. The result is to the benefit of everyone involved: students, teachers, and parents.

CHAPTER 10

COMPETENCY # 10: BUILD KIDS' CHARACTER

Parents are able to build into the lives of their children the character traits that they will need to achieve academic success.

"I believe that many Latino students don't do well in school because they just live for today, you know, like there is no tomorrow. They would rather work many hours so they can buy that new phone or expensive pair of sneakers. If you want that better future you really need to 'de veras hecharle ganas a los studios' [Truly put effort into studying]. *You can't give up no matter how hard things get. I know that my mom is always on my case, telling me that I have to push hard and become somebody because that is why she brought me to this country."* — Roberto, Hispanic High School Student

COMPETENCY # 10: BUILDS KIDS' CHARACTER

I am sure that you will agree with me that people's characters are behind their actions. Actions are what we do, but our character traits (who we are) determine why we do them. For students to consistently exhibit conduct that supports academic success, parents must build character traits in their children that will drive the desired behaviors. Parents are in the driver's seat when it comes to their kids' education. They are responsible for ensuring that their children receive a quality education and a big part of this role is teaching their children the character traits that are needed to excel in school. Parents must take this role seriously. And, we must hold them accountable for doing so. This is why I believe that parents' ability to build in their children the character traits that are conducive to academic success must be one of the competencies they must demonstrate.

Out of the many positive character traits linked to academic success, I teach four traits that I consider significant to achieving success in school. They are responsibility, a smart-hard work ethic, persistence, and the ability to delay personal gratification. Students that exhibit these character traits are in "cruise control." Let me use a personal example to explain what I mean by this.

I have raised three children. Two of them have already earned four-year college degrees. The youngest will graduate this year. Believe

me, school was hard work for them, just as it is for most immigrant students. There were challenging times during their academic journeys in which I had to steer them to focus on their studies or implement new strategies to complete assignments or projects. While sitting in the driver's seat, I taught them how to behave in a responsible manner, the great benefits of a smart-hard work ethics, the value of persisting and never giving up, and how rewarding giving up immediate gratification can be. It was not easy, but it was worth it! I did not have to press the accelerator all the time because these character traits set them on cruise control. My three children had personal internal motivations for doing well in school. Their motivation to pursue academic excellence was born out of these four character traits they developed. How can parents teach these character traits to their children?

Children may develop character traits that are conducive to academic success by seeing them demonstrated by others. However, parents who understand how important it is will not leave their children to figure them out on their own. The parents must be role models and teachers of these traits to their children. William Bennett, former United States Secretary of Education, states, "If we want our children to possess the traits of character we most admire, we need to teach them what those traits are."

I also teach parents that they must give these character traits a name, especially when they are manifested in their children's behaviors or actions. Character traits are abstract concepts. It is very difficult to learn a concept that does not have a name. For example, instead of simply saying "Good job" when a child does homework without being told, the parent could say, "Good job. You really showed me responsibility." Suddenly, the parent is giving a name to the character trait, identifying the "why" behind the action, and rewarding the child through praise for the character trait that produced the right action - doing homework without being told. Here I discuss the four character traits that I focus on when I train parents.

CHARACTER TRAIT # 1: RESPONSIBILITY

The first of the four character traits that I link to academic success is responsibility. Parents must teach their children responsibility because sooner or later their children will be held accountable for tasks at home, school, work, or church.

When children behave in a responsible manner, they do not let people down. If they agree to do something, they do it. Students who have learned responsibility hold themselves accountable for their own actions. They do not make excuses or blame others for what they did or did not do. Students whose actions demonstrate responsibility take care of their personal matters. They do not rely on their parents or other people for things they are supposed to do themselves. Students who have developed this very important character trait follow guidelines and meet due dates. They do what they have to do in school on time and follow instructions; they do not cut corners.

It is wonderful to teach students who have developed this

character trait. Their responsibility is manifested in their actions during and after the school day. For example, if José agreed to meet his peers at the school library after school, he will be there even if he gets invited to do something more fun. If Rosa did not study and failed a test, she will not say, "The teacher never covered that material in class." If Carlos has to do some research about a certain topic, he will not ask or allow any of his peers to do the work for him. If Maria has to turn in a paper on a certain day, she will not "get sick" just to avoid seeing the teacher that day.

I teach parents that children can also demonstrate responsibility when they serve others. I believe that we can all have greater significance in our lives when we are part of something greater than ourselves. Serving others gives people a purpose in life. Dr. Albert Einstein said, "Most people say that it is the intellect which makes a great scientist. They are wrong. It is character."

CHARACTER TRAIT # 2: A SMART-HARD WORK-ETHIC

The second of the four character traits is a smart-hard work ethic. Parents need to teach their children to value both a smart and a hard kind of effort. Working hard is important, but working smart is even more important. I have seen too many students, and even adults, putting an enormous amount of effort into goals without any results. They might be aiming at the right thing but in a wrong way.

When students exhibit a smart-hard work ethic, they have a

clear understanding of their academic goals. It is very difficult to reach competency in any academic subject without a clear understanding of the goals that must be reached to get to that level of proficiency. For example, if Carlos, a high school student, wants to be accepted to an elite engineering program, he must have a clear understand of the math courses he is required to pass in order to be considered for acceptance.

Students, who have a smart-hard work ethics, believe that they have what it takes to reach their academic goals. It is difficult to reach proficiency in any academic subject if the belief that it can be accomplished is not there. For example, Joe is likely to enroll in an AP Calculus class if he believes he has what it takes to successfully pass the course. Joe's belief in his ability will boost the confidence needed to achieve his goals.

Students who practice a smart-hard work ethic are committed to do whatever it takes to reach academic proficiency. It is difficult to put effort into an academic subject when the commitment is not there. For example, if George is committed to passing the Physics class with an A, he is willing to spend time to do homework, participate in class and study for the tests, instead of spending his time engaged in distractions. He is committed. He is serious!

CHARACTER TRAIT # 3: PERSISTENCE

Persistence is the third character trait that I ask parents to teach their children. People who have this character trait usually also have a strong work ethic. When confronted with challenges, people who are persistent do not give up because they have an internal motivation to keep on going. You have heard the expression, "When the going gets tough, the tough gets going."

Persistence is a character trait that, like the others, needs to be taught. Persistence is not hereditary; it is learned. For example, almost all parents, at one time or another, have to re-direct their children back to their homework. This especially applies to families in which getting kids to do their homework is a daily battle instead of a daily routine.

When children struggle with their homework, parents can make it a "character education moment." Instead of telling their children again and again to do their homework, they can talk to their children about the meaning of persistence, explain to their children why this character trait is so important in their academic careers, and let their children know that they expect them to learn to be persistent.

Parents can tie rewards to character traits. For example, instead of rewarding their children for doing their school work, parents must reward their children for demonstrating persistence by overcoming challenges and not giving up. They are being taught persistence by having the character trait name attached to the desired behavior and then having that trait affirmed. It is also important that parents do not tell their children, "You're not persistent," rather, affirm them with statements like "I believe, I know, and I expect you to develop persistence."

CHARACTER TRAIT # 4: ABILITY TO DELAY PERSONAL GRATIFICATION

The last, but not least of the character traits that parents must teach their children is the ability to delay personal gratification. As I said before, parents are in the "driver's seat" when it comes to guiding their children's academic and character development. A significant part of this role is teaching their children the ability to wait – to not seek instantaneous indulgence when pursuing their academic goals.

Some people are almost slaves to whatever thing, activity, person, etc. that brings immediate gratification. Sad, isn't it? But, the reality is that most of the things that are valuable in life require sacrifice. Delayed gratification is an invaluable character trait because it gives the individual the ability to give up immediate pleasure for long-term benefits. This character trait is demonstrated when students have the will to delay the fun of playing video games or talking with their friends, until they have completed all their homework assignments.

For example, parents can help develop this trait when they talk to their children about something their children want to buy (like a new CD) or something they want to do (like going to the movies with their friends). Parents can help their children establish academic goals they want to achieve for that week or month. Finally, they can reward their children for their own achievements by buying that CD or taking them and their friends to the movies. Most of all, sooner than later, students must learn this magnificent character trait. It is a sacrifice to deny yourself from immediate gratification. But, the greater the goal, the greater the sacrifice will be.

A young woman brought her baby son to Robert E. Lee, the well-known Confederate general. She asked him what she should do to help her son succeed, to which Robert E. Lee replied, "Teach him to deny himself."

We can see this character trait in all our great athletes. None of them have reached greatness without painful practices and sore muscles. The pain they feel because of their hard work is like a badge of honor.

It is imperative that we teach parents the importance and the process of developing the character traits of responsibility, a smart-hard work ethic, persistence and the ability to delay personal gratification. Students who exhibit these character traits are more likely to achieve academic success than those who do not. Helping children develop these traits puts their academic achievement on cruise control.

With the internal motivation to do well, they are self-propelled. Developing these traits in children is possible. I personally expect all Hispanic parents to do so. Once we have provided parents and students with the tools they need, we must expect them to use them. Character will drive them to a quality education and a quality life.

Closing Thoughts

CLOSING THOUGHTS

Hopefully, you've gained some valuable insights into the issue of Hispanic parental involvement in this book. In my presentation to Hispanic parents, I always tell them "You are in the driver's seat." We must help them get there. As educators we should design and implement parental involvement programs that help Hispanic parents reach the ten competencies that I have presented in this book.

It is important that we all understand that we need to create the right environment to implement these programs. There are three conditions that must be met to ensure that the Hispanic parental involvement programs you offer are a success.

The first condition is that you and your staff express great love and appreciation for our nation in an unapologetic and fresh way. We need to pass that appreciation on to Hispanic families. I am grieved by the constant criticism that I hear in the media about our nation. I am completely aware of the mistakes that we have made, but this is our country. In spite of our past mistakes, the U.S. is still the best nation in the world. During my seminars I always share with the participants that, "This is the only ship I have. So, I am determined to make it stronger and better. If the ship sinks, my three siblings, my three children, my three grandchildren and I will go down with it." So, making our nation stronger and more competitive in this global and highly technological economy must be a priority, especially for those of us in charge of cultivating our greatest national asset, our children.

The second condition that must be met is a clear understanding that Hispanics are the largest and fastest growing minority in the United States. We must admit that this unique sector of our population has brought our nation new challenges, and among the greatest is meeting the academic needs of Hispanic students. Helping these students achieve academic success must be a priority in our schools' reform efforts. Because parental involvement is one of the leading conditions for students' academic success, establishing programs to get more parents involved in their kids' education must be at the top of our list of our school improvement goals. We need to move away from "tolerance." Tolerating Hispanics will not help Hispanic students achieve.

We must move away from "celebrating diversity." Celebrating diversity can improve the schools' climate, but not necessarily actualize Hispanic academic success. Instead of tolerating or celebrating, we must tap into their huge potential of this unique population. Hispanics are people who value family, have a strong work-ethic and hold on to their faith for reaching a better life. I believe the United States needs a dose of family unity, a dose of hard-work versus entitlement, and most of all, a heavy dose of faith; faith that we can build a better future for our grandchildren. Fifty-plus millions of Hispanic people are not going to disappear. So, let's tap into their potential and make our nation stronger.

The third and last of the condition that must be met is that you and your staff accept the challenge of reaching out to the Hispanic community. You do not have to be Hispanic to reach out to the Hispanic community? You do not need to be competent in the Spanish language to invest time, energy, and resources into needed programs. If you are not Hispanic, hire Hispanic staff members who are highly proficient in the Spanish language and have a deep understanding of the Hispanic culture. They will be pivotal in the planning process and your right hand when implementing any Hispanic outreach program. You must learn as much as you can about the Hispanic culture including language, beliefs, values and traditions. During one of your vacation times, visit any of the Latin American countries. I promise you will love it, especially if you go to Puerto Rico. Don't forget that I am Puerto Rican. Once in a while, listen to a Hispanic radio station, watch a Hispanic TV show, visit a Hispanic church service or attend a Hispanic social event. If you enjoy dancing like me, take some Latin dance classes. And most of all, try to make friends with some Hispanic folks. If you show interest in getting to know them, they will embrace you. You will definitely get invited to some quinceañera parties.

Not long ago, during one of my parental involvement seminars, a Caucasian school administrator said to me, "I feel there is nothing I can do to get more parents involved. I am white and my Spanish is far from good. Would they (parents) listen to me?"

I paused for a minute, because her questions took me by surprise, and she looked pretty concerned. To her questions I responded, "Do you understand the American Educational System?"

Her response was "yes." "Have you been successful in school?" She responded with another "yes." "Do you care about the academic achievement of Hispanic students?" She passionately responded with another "yes." "Do you believe in their potential to reach a quality life in the United States?" To this last question she responded with an even louder "yes."

Turning to the entire group I addressed them with the following words,

Navigating the American Educational System is almost like crossing a dense jungle. All of you know this jungle in and out. You know every path to take and every danger to avoid. So, you are the experts. Help students and their parents successfully cross to the other side where a better future awaits. You are the right person to get them through.

I love the United States of America. This is my nation! I also believe in the God-given potential that Hispanics have to make our nation stronger than ever. I also believe that you, no matter your race or ethnicity or level of Spanish proficiency, can help this sector of our population improve the quality of their lives and contribute to the welfare of our great nation.

I pray that this book will motivate you to think out of the box and boldly establish programs that can teach parents each of these ten competencies so they "sit in the driver's seat" and take their children to their final academic destination.

Bueno, ahí me despido de cada uno de ustedes. Ahí nos vemos amigos.

ABOUT THE AUTHOR

ABOUT THE AUTHOR

Growing up in a disadvantaged family in Puerto Rico, Lourdes soon learned that education was the way out of the poverty cycle. This understanding led her to complete her undergraduate degree in mathematics and begin teaching. She left Puerto Rico in 1979 to do community development work in Guatemala. She established and directed schools, an orphanage, feeding centers, and clinics. She procured resources for these entities through interaction with non-profit organizations and by obtaining assistance from Guatemalan government officials. Her community education work consisted of educational radio programs and parent education in various venues. Her experience in community development was a catalyst that led Lourdes to choose Research, Evaluation, and Measurement as the focus of her Master's degree.

When she moved to the United States in 1990, she had to overcome enormous financial, linguistic, and cultural barriers to pursue the American Dream. She first worked as a Middle School Bilingual Curriculum Content (BCC) mathematics teacher in Dade County and then as Regular High School mathematics teacher in Palm Beach County.

She went on to complete her Ed.D in Leadership and took a position as a School Improvement and Assessment Specialist for the School District of Palm Beach County. Her responsibilities included leading NCLB staff development opportunities for teachers and school administrators, as well as speaking at community forums regarding the same issues.

Dr. Lourdes is an Education Consultant, Public Speaker and Researcher who assists districts and schools to create data streams through quantitative or qualitative studies. She utilizes programs, methods, and strategies to train teachers, administrators, district personnel, students, parents and the communities at large, to help minority students achieve academic proficiency.

She provides consulting services, staff development opportunities, and motivational speaking. Her seminars include: School culture, Hispanic and African American academic achievement, parental involvement, assessment literacy, assessment development, test-taking strategies, data analysis, goals setting, student motivation, team-building, , and mathematics content by strands.

In order to have a better understanding of the lack of achievement among minority students Dr. Lourdes has been interviewing hundreds of English Language Learner (ELL), Hispanic, African- American and Native American middle and high school students to find out, from their perspective, what are the underlying reasons for their lack of achievement and what can the school do to help them improve. These findings are used to customize strategic plans at the school level to help the target population.

Dr. Lourdes is the author of "Navigating the American Educational System (NAES): A Curricular and Training Hispanic

Parental Involvement" program. The purpose of this program is to increase Hispanic academic achievement through increased parental involvement. This program provides bilingual educators, social workers, psychologists and community liaison the knowledge and skills they need to conduct successful parent workshops in Spanish. Nearly 500 participants have completed this program and are currently conducting numerous parent workshops throughout the state of Illinois. She went on to create a program called "In the Driver's Seat" which includes resources and videos on the ten competencies Hispanic parents need to improve their children's academic success.

Made in the USA
Middletown, DE
17 October 2017